THE HAWAII HOME BOOK

PRACTICAL TIPS *for* TROPICAL LIVING

KAREN ANDERSON

WATERMARK
PUBLISHING

ISBN-10: 0-9753740-9-5
ISBN-13: 978-0-9753740-9-2

Library of Congress Control Number:
20066923445

Design/Production: Gonzalez Design

Watermark Publishing
1088 Bishop Street, Suite 310
Honolulu, HI 96813
Telephone: Toll-free 1-866-900-BOOK
Web site: www.bookshawaii.net
e-mail: sales@bookshawaii.net

Printed in Korea

Contents

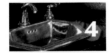

Introduction

E komo mai...welcome to the challenges, and rewards, of life in the Hawaiian Islands!

A few years back, I was living in an old beach house on the Big Island of Hawaii. Located in a South Kona subdivision—an area listed as Lava Zone 2—the home was decidedly the worse for wear. The metal roof was rusting, exterior paint chipping, railings on the lanai warped and loose, pipes corroded and the trim riddled with termites. Menacing wasps built nests in the eaves, and centipedes lurked beyond the doors. Living on catchment water was a challenge; my hair always felt filmy after a shower. The small propane tank for heating water offered little more than a month's worth of fuel, while the pilot light on the Paloma often flickered out in the breeze. My new tools quickly rusted beyond recognition, and the salt air wreaked havoc on the screens and windows.

Yet what could beat living so close to the water, with a beautiful view of the pebble beach and the sound of the ocean lulling me to sleep at night? Ah, paradise! I love living in Hawaii, challenges be damned.

Up the road 1,000 feet in elevation, my sister and her family of four had their share of homeowner problems. The millipedes that didn't exist on my street were out in droves on hers, entering both levels of the house any way they could during their seasonal march to God-knows-where. In the ongoing drought, their catchment tank always seemed near empty. One day, many of the cheap pressboard cabinet doors, shelves and drawers—in their otherwise beautiful and contemporary kitchen—simply fell apart from the humidity. Mold worked its way through the drywall near a leak in the bathroom pipes, dry-rotting the adjacent antique furniture. The next-door neighbors were far too close for comfort, yet nobody thought to plant tall hedges to block their proximity. My sister's home office was inundated with more nesting geckos than most people see in a lifetime. The monthly electricity bill was astronomical.

Yet their lovely Island house, with its 180-degree view of the South Kona Coast, was home sweet home. They wouldn't have dreamed of living anywhere else.

Adapting to a tropical environment can be a major learning experience. From confronting the elements like mold and corrosion to choosing the best type of construction materials for your pool deck, the challenges of Island life are ever present—whether you're a renter or homeowner, kamaaina or malihini, or snowbird or other mainlander dreaming of owning your own slice of paradise.

This book offers residents helpful tips and advice specific to living in Hawaii. Much of the information contained herein evolved with the assistance of seasoned experts in their respective fields. Some of the tidbits—like how best to smash a centipede or how to effectively prevent millipedes from entering your home—are passed down from trusted locals whose best remedies to these problems come from personal experience.

In researching this book, I quickly discovered several recurring themes. First and foremost, you get what you pay for. Opting for that low-end pool pump, cheap house paint or bargain-basement ceiling fan will only cost you money in the long run when it comes time to replace, refinish or redo. The other common denominator is the sun—how best to protect your assets from its damaging UV rays? The tropical sun, it seems, knows no boundaries when it comes to affecting your pool deck, hardwood flooring, roof, exterior finish, outdoor lighting, lanai, fish pond, landscaping or bamboo tiki hut, not to mention the valued furniture and artwork inside your home.

While some homeowner topics like windows, screens and paint might appear generic to any homeowner's manual, the fact is, there's always something specific or peculiar to Hawaii to be taken into account. What works on the mainland doesn't necessarily work in the Islands. You might have an excellent gardening background in California, for example, but the learning curve in Hawaii presents new and exciting challenges for even the most seasoned green thumb. Exterior paint can require extra fortification depending on your elevation. Swimming pool maintenance is an entirely unique scenario.

Just about every endeavor involving the home takes on special significance in Hawaii, whether you live in a coffee shack or a multi-million-dollar estate. Pests, mold, corrosion and heat do not discriminate. Nor does the sun. If you're a newcomer, you'll learn a lot of it the hard way. If you're a longtime resident, there's always something new to learn. That's why I wrote this book—to help make life just a little easier, so that you can enjoy your Hawaii home to the fullest. It's my hope that you'll find the information in these pages to be practical, helpful, informative and, most of all, relevant. You'll also find the information easy on the eyes, thanks in part to some beautiful images from the photographers of *Hawaii Home + Remodeling* magazine

So pull up a plastic chair, sit back on your termite-ridden lanai, slap a few skeeters and begin at the beginning—with The Basics.

Aloha,
Karen Anderson

The Basics

Construction Styles in Hawaii

Homebuilding in Hawaii encompasses various styles, each with its own attributes. From post-and-pier construction to pole houses, most Island homes reflect Hawaii's unique tropical environment.

POST-AND-PIER

A big part of Hawaii's architectural landscape, post-and-pier homes are ideal for the tropics. Along with a view, a post-and-pier home gives you distance from the bugs outside, as well as allowing for increased airflow to keep things drier and to prevent mold and mildew.

Post-and-pier construction involves building a home off the ground on posts fitted into concrete foundations or "piers." Many people opt for post-and-pier because they gain space beneath the house for storage, a garage or an add-on. Plus, a wood floor is easier on the knees than concrete!

Post-and-pier is suited for areas that are steep or prone to rock slides or flooding. It's also preferable to be off the ground if you are on the oceanfront. No matter your location, however, there may be county, state or subdivision restrictions on how high you can build.

In the last few decades, changes in building codes have made for safer post-and-pier construction methods in Hawaii. Today, the post is set into the concrete block and bolted down through a series of bolts and hardware that secures the structure in a continuous tie all the way up to the roof. The house is as strong as all of the components combined.

Many older post-and-pier homes built in Hawaii were built on "tofu blocks." Take one look at a house on tofu blocks and you'll see the precariousness of the situation. Amazingly, the post is resting only on top of a concrete block, and that's it. During an earthquake, a house on tofu blocks can actually "walk" off the piers because nothing is holding it to the ground. Homeowners should definitely retrofit a post-and-pier foundation if the structure was built more than 25 years ago or if it is built on tofu blocks.

SLAB-ON-GRADE

Slab-on-grade begins with a concrete pour that serves as the floor. This style of construction works well if the house is on a knoll or a flat house site. Because you can start framing immediately, slab-on-grade homes are quicker to build than post-and-

The varied eave heights and railings make this post-and-pier house look much larger than its actual square footage.

pier. They are also generally less expensive because there are less materials and labor involved.

Slab-on-grade provides a solid foundation. The outer edge is thicker than the center so that it will accommodate the weight of the walls bearing down on it. Although slab-on-grade is considered less costly than post-and-pier, costs will vary depending on the size of the house, the location, the contractor's expertise and the homeowner's requirements. Some homes feature a combination of slab-on-grade and post-and-pier.

The soil beneath the slab must be pre-treated for termites.

POLE HOUSES

Originating in Japan and Polynesia, the pole house style of architecture is truly unique and perfectly suited to Hawaii. In a pole house, large wood poles bear the entire load of the home, while the walls bear none of the weight. Measuring at least 12 inches in diameter and set into a concrete footing, poles can be made of cedar, Douglas fir, ironwood, ohia, lodgepole pine, eucalyptus robusta and other types of hardwood. Ohia posts, while more expensive and difficult to use than some of the others, add a distinctive Hawaiian look to the pole house.

The number of poles depends on the size and design of the home. Typically the poles are part of the exterior, but they can also be erected inside the house. The poles rise vertically through the entire structure to carry the suspended floor girder beams, joists and roofing rafters, making for an exceptionally strong frame. Because the walls are completely non-load bearing, there is more freedom to place walls anywhere you want, or to reconfigure entire rooms at any time.

Pole houses can be more economical to build because there is no need to excavate the site or build retaining walls, plus you can build on terrain that might otherwise be considered too difficult.

Building a pole house takes less material than conventional homebuilding, and it can be quicker. The simplicity of construction makes the pole house a great option for the owner/builder.

KIT HOMES

Kit or "packaged" homes are popular in Hawaii. Stores like Trojan, HPM and Honsador Lumber all sell kit homes in a variety of designs, sizes and amenities. There are also companies that sell

Pole houses are constructed with poles that bear the entire weight of the house. Because the walls bear none of the weight, they can be reconfigured at a later date if you want to change the size or layout of a room.

prefab bamboo hales, yurts, pole houses and just about anything you can think of in every price range.

If you want to expand or modify the existing design, upgrade options such as nicer fixtures, lighting, countertops, etc., are usually available. Some packages even come complete with appliances like dishwashers, washing machines and dryers. There is quite a bit of leeway to add another room if you desire.

When choosing a company, it's best to go with one that will bond the job. That way you'll be in a better position to acquire a loan from the bank. Hire a surveyor to help you choose the right home to suit your lot. When it's time to start building, you'll want the materials delivered piecemeal rather than all at once so that you can finish one section before you start on the next. You don't want to have a mountainload of material sitting out tempting would-be thieves or getting exposed to the elements.

ASPHALT SHINGLES

Asphalt shingles have come a long way since the old days when they were known to fail in Hawaii. Composite asphalt shingles are made to be algae resistant so that they don't get black and ugly. They are also relatively affordable to have installed, especially the three-tab shingle.

The higher-end asphalt shingles are laminated for more depth. Because asphalt-shingle roofing has fiberglass and chemicals in it, it should not be used to catch water.

CLAY AND CEMENT TILES

Among the highest-end products in the roofing industry, concrete and clay tiles need to be installed properly so that they hold up in high winds. Clay tiles rarely fade. Concrete tile roofs are popular in Hawaii.

Japanese glazed tile roofs are especially upscale, showcasing bright greens and royal blues with ornate trim.

Wood shake offers a natural look and lots of character, plus great insulation for keeping the house cool. Shake roofs perform well in wet elevations.

SHAKE

When it comes to keeping your house cool, cedar shake is the gold standard, providing great insulation against heat. Traditionally, regular linseed oil treatments were recommended for shake roofs. Today, the cedar shake mills assert there is no real reconditioning process for cedar shakes other than keeping them clean of debris. In Hawaii, a shake roof performs best in wet elevations and is not particularly suited for drier areas.

IRONWOOD SHINGLES

A wood shingle that can be made to look like thatch, the ironwood shingle holds up very well against dry rot, mildew and termites. A high-end product in the price range of tile or copper roofing, ironwood shingles come in two styles: the re-sawn "smooth" kind or the hand-split kind with a rough texture that looks like real thatch. If installed properly with stainless steel fasteners, these shingles are touted to last 50 years and up. Their insulating properties will keep heat out of the house.

SIMULATED THATCH

Undoubtedly one of the most expensive roofs in Hawaii, simulated thatch is made of PVC or polyurethane and comes in two styles: coco palm and reed. How expensive, you ask? About $1,600 per square, or $16 per square foot.

A WORD ABOUT WARRANTIES

READ the fine print. Despite claiming to have a 30-, 40- or 50-year warranty, some manufacturers might not actually cover such basic problems as leakage, color fade or breakage. According to a recent class-action lawsuit won against the makers of Cal-Shake fiber cement roofing, the manufacturer's warranty was baseless and the product was failing. From 1980 to 1995, Cal-Shake roofs were sold and installed on more than 32,000 homes or buildings in Hawaii. A $61.4 million settlement was announced in 2005.

ROOF-MAINTENANCE TIPS

• KEEP YOUR ROOF CLEAN OF LEAVES AND DEBRIS THAT CAN CAUSE MOISTURE DAMAGE, ROT, MOLD AND CORROSION.

• KEEP TREES TRIMMED AND BRANCHES A GOOD DISTANCE FROM THE ROOF.

• MAKE SURE GUTTERS, DOWN-SPOUTS AND ROOF DRAINS ARE FREE OF DEBRIS.

• BLACK STREAKS ON THE ROOF INDICATE MOLD, WHICH WILL EVENTUALLY EAT AWAY AT THE ROOF AND ENTER YOUR HOME.

• WHEN INSPECTING YOUR ROOF, ALSO LOOK FOR MOISTURE STAINS ON YOUR CEILINGS AND THE UNDERSIDE OF EAVES, AND AT THE FASCIA. BE SAFE. INSPECT FROM THE GROUND OR ON A LADDER.

• HIRE A CERTIFIED HOME INSPECTOR OR ROOFING CONTRACTOR WHEN YOU NEED A THOROUGH AND SAFE INSPECTION OF YOUR ROOF.

Hardwood Flooring

A wood floor can be the defining element of the home, influencing everything from your choice of furniture to trim and wall color.

Mahalo for removing your shoes!
If you're like most people in Hawaii, going barefoot inside your home is standard operating procedure. Therefore, the floor that comes in close contact with the feet takes on special significance in an Island home.

FLOORED!

Not only does a gorgeous hardwood floor provide lasting beauty for your home's interior, wood is a lot easier on your knees and hips than tile or slab. In Hawaii's humid environment, wood is also more practical than carpeting, which can attract mold and mildew and aggravate allergies.

Whether dark or light, exotic or domestic, a wood floor can be the defining element of the home, influencing everything from your choice of furnishings, window treatments and trim to the color of your walls and the cabinetry you choose. These days, owners of higher-end Hawaii homes are opting for richly hued, darker floors like Brazilian cherry and jarrah, in chocolate browns, reds and dark browns. Even coconut, a softer exotic wood, features a deep brownish-red color with a spotty black grain.

Wood flooring from left to right: teak, maple, tigerwood, bamboo, merbau, oak and pyinkaod.

Native tropical hardwoods popular for flooring include ohia, monkeypod and mango—a "sleeper" wood with a swirling amber luminescence that's gaining popularity in the Islands. Due its expense and scarcity, koa is now rare for flooring applications. Koala wood from Australia is a koa look-alike priced at less than half the cost.

Cork is a renewable resource now being used for flooring. It is soft underfoot and provides excellent sound insulation. Highly affordable, bamboo is another renewable resource that features a real tropical look. Bamboo flooring comes in different stains and graining but can be difficult to install due to its tendency to splinter. Teak is a softer, oily wood that looks fantastic as flooring, but it's expensive and sometimes resistant to finishing.

WEAR, OH, WEAR...

Like many people, you may have a particular wood in mind before making a purchase. You saw it at a friend's house or in a magazine, or a decorator suggested it. But the question remains: how wear-resistant will the flooring be?

It is a fallacy to think that putting five coats of finish on your wood floor will help it wear better. It may wear *longer*, but the finish won't prevent dings or scratches.

The fact is, the harder the hardwood, the less likely it is to dent. You can drop a knife or a pan on the harder types and they

Cork comes in a variety of colors, is soft underfoot and provides excellent sound insulation.

might ding, but not as easily or as deeply as oak or bamboo. Of all the hardwood materials, Brazilian ebony is the hardest of the hard—capturing the top spot on the "crush point" scale at 3,692 pounds per square inch (psi). Brazilian cherry follows closely at 3,650 psi.

Sunlight is the biggest enemy of Hawaii hardwood floors. Wood will discolor over time—beginning as early as three to six months. All of the exotic floors change color when exposed to sunlight, Brazilian cherry and Brazilian ebony included. With UV streaming down upon it, Brazilian ebony can lose its nice milk-chocolate color and turn black. Maple will change from a buttery white to a burnt-brown-sugar color.

You can slow down the process to some degree with tinted windows or UV-filtering window film, but there is little hope of inhibiting the effects altogether when sunlight enters the home.

Moving day is another potential trauma for a hardwood floor. Sliding heavy pieces of furniture across the room will leave scratches. Combine that with a dolly and a couple of hurried movers, and you have a recipe for permanent damage. Put soft, protective glides on the legs of all your furniture to prevent scuffing and scratching. Be sure to clean or change the glides regularly, as dirt and sand can become embedded in them.

WHAT ELSE CAN DAMAGE A HARDWOOD FLOOR?

• **Water**—Wet-mopping or excessive water will cause the grain to rise and the wood to expand, crack or splinter. Don't clean your wood floors with water!

• **Oils, soaps and ammonias**—Theoretically, anything that leaves a residue is not good for a wood floor, because you'll have a hard time removing it and getting another coat of finish to bond to the original finish. Don't use products like Murphy's Oil, Pledge, Mop & Glo and other products that will harm the performance of your floor. Ammonias like Formula 409 can also dull or damage the wood.

• **Clueless housecleaners**—If you have a housecleaner, make darn sure you know exactly how s/he's cleaning your hardwood floor. General sweeping and vacuuming will suffice for weekly maintenance.

• **High heels**—Heels with no protective cap or shoes with exposed sharp hardware will exert up to 8,000 pounds per square inch of pressure on the floor, enough to damage any floor, no matter the material.

• **Dogs**—Oils from your dog's skin can damage a floor. Try not to let your dog sleep in the same place for long periods of time—unless it's on a dog bed.

MAINTENANCE TIPS

How to clean a hardwood floor? Industry experts highly recommend "Bona Swedish Formula Hardwood Floor Cleaner" from BonaKemi, a company that's been in the hardwood flooring business for 75 years. The cleaner is nontoxic and waterborne, and it will not leave a residue or dull your finish. Apply it directly to the floor and wipe with a terry cloth Swiffer™ once a month, or when needed for spills.

To treat a scratch, you can try dabbing on finish with a Q-tip or fine painter's brush, but there's no quick remedy to make it go away unless you sand down the floor and do it over again. If it's a pre-finished floor, you may be able to replace the board, but it could be costly. Additionally, there's a good chance that the scratch will be going across the grain, which means you'll need to replace boards in a row instead of in a line.

Wood floors are not inert; they move with moisture and contract with dryness. As floors continue to move, there will be some microscopic cracks within your finish. That's another reason why manufacturers don't want you to use water or oil to clean your floor. Oil will actually get into the grain and act as a wick. Even if you try to buff and finish the area, you could get an opalescent spot where the finish will have problems adhering, resulting in a fisheye effect.

Sometimes a hardwood floor becomes so dark, the actual species of wood is unrecognizable. Refinishing a hardwood floor involves sanding off the original finish and applying a new one, a process that could take three to four days, depending on the contractor. The results can be absolutely stunning. It's not cheap, but it's cheaper than installing carpet or a new hardwood floor.

ALWAYS CLIMATIZE YOUR FLOORING

With Hawaii's high humidity, it's especially important to make sure your wood flooring material is acclimated to the moisture level of your home site before it's installed. Most wood for floors is kilned down and dried out to about six or seven percent moisture. Thus there's a big disparity in its moisture content and that of your

Dark hardwood flooring is the new, upscale choice in Hawaii over the lighter-colored woods.

A softer wood, mango has an amber quality that brings lightness and a luminescent ambiance to a tropical home. Below: With dark hardwoods, tropical touches and open-air breezes, this bedroom suite has the look and feel of an upscale resort.

home's environment. If you don't allow the wood to expand, it will grow in width and sometimes thickness, depending on the cut, which could result in warping or buckling once installed. Wood should be within three to four moisture points of the subfloor.

It takes months and months to climatize most woods, ideally up to a year. This is admittedly impractical for many homeowners, but believe your flooring contractor when he tells you to climatize your wood—it's not just a lame excuse to stall on your project. If you can place the wood in your garage and let it breathe for a minimum of five months before it's installed, you will be dollars ahead in the long run. If your home is under construction, you can put the wood in a trailer with an air vent and let it sit while the house is being built.

Acclimation is particularly important with solids, whether pre-finished or unfinished. Because they are sealed at the top, pre-finished solids will climatize faster than unfinished solids, which will draw moisture from top to bottom. Engineered floors are cross-laminated and therefore need only to acclimate between 24 and 72 hours, depending on manufacturer. Kit floors from big-box retailers should also be climatized.

Windows

Does your picture window fully capture that big, beautiful view you could be enjoying? Are you getting as much ventilation as you'd like? Maybe you have too much sun coming through a particular window, or rain and water are somehow getting in? What about security?

When choosing the right windows for the Hawaii home, there are many factors to consider. No matter the situation, there is a style of window, an architectural remedy or a specialty product that will provide a solution.

Skylights not only release trapped hot air and let cool air in, they also diffuse light evenly throughout the room.

HEAT AND CORROSION—WHAT A PANE

In a tropical environment, corrosion is a fact of life. But it doesn't have to impact your windows. Vinyl windows are an excellent choice in Hawaii because they hold up well against corrosion, especially vinyl windows manufactured specifically for the tropics.

With vinyl windows, the frames, grids and tracks are made of specially formulated vinyl that withstands the harsh climate. It's important to note that the quality of the vinyl differs from manufacturer to manufacturer, so choose a brand of vinyl window that's been proven in the tropics. Do your research based on what your needs are and what will best fit those needs. Vinyl windows are ideally suited to Hawaii. Sliding windows that ride on Teflon strips are made with minimum hardware for maximum corrosion prevention.

Heat is another factor. When designing your home, orient your biggest windows under the roof overhangs for as much shade as possible. The sun is higher in the sky to the north and lower in the sky to the south, so make sure the overhangs are built accordingly. Windows on the north or south side are easiest to shade, while west-facing windows tend to take in a lot of afternoon sun that is difficult to block.

White vinyl frames will reflect the sun and stay cooler, as opposed to aluminum frames, which gather heat. Tinted window glass of various shades also offers solar control. Blue-green, gray and bronze tints work the best. Double-paned glass, also known as insulated glass, is the most heat resistant, but it can actually make the house hotter if the air conditioning is turned off and the house is all sealed up. There is no way for the interior heat to escape. For existing windows, tinted plastic film can be applied to reduce heat.

TIP: The orientation of your house should dictate your window placement. Think about your home's positioning as it relates to the flow of the trade winds, the direction of the afternoon sun and the likelihood of wind-driven rain.

JUST VENTING

You can harness the breeze to ventilate your home. For maximum ventilation, you need a combination of good window positioning, a good-sized opening and the right style of window.

Security jalousies are made with tamper-proof clips to keep louvers firmly in place.

Survey the general direction of the breeze or trade winds in your neighborhood. Does the cool wind blow mauka-makai at night? Do you get an onshore breeze? From which direction do the trade winds come?

When considering where to put your openings, a 45-degree orientation to the direction of the wind is best. In general, the area for a window opening should be about 12 percent of the floor area it serves. Certain window types can increase your airflow. With casement windows, for example, you can actually direct airflow in and out of your house.

Jalousie, awning and casement windows provide the most ventilation. Each style is used widely throughout the Islands.

Awning windows are hinged at the top and crank open vertically, allowing tropical breezes in while keeping rain out.

Jalousie windows

A jalousie window, also known as a louvered window, offers ventilation when fully opened. The window is operated with a crank or lever that tilts a series of horizontal louvers inward, allowing the breezes to flow through. Louvers can be made of glass, wood or vinyl.

Standard aluminum jalousies are easy to break into and are therefore a security risk. Security jalousies feature solid vinyl frames and tamper-proof clips that cannot be bent. The vinyl-slat jalousies are even more secure because the slats are screwed onto the actual hardware.

Jalousies serve well as primary windows, but you'll also often see smaller venting jalousies installed above or below picture windows or doors for increased airflow.

Awning windows

The awning window is hinged at the top and cranks up horizontally like a flap. You can get single-vent or double-vent awnings, or even have the windows stacked in groups of three or more. An awning window can remain open and still offer protection against a light rain. Not all brands of awning windows open to the full 90 degrees, so if you want increased flexibility and more airflow, check the manufacturer's specifications ahead of time.

Casement windows are hinged at the side and crank open horizontally so you can redirect cool trade winds and draw them into the house.

Casement windows

Casement windows are hinged at the side and crank open from left to right or vice-versa. If you position the pane at a given angle, you can direct the trade winds for the desired ventilation into your home, all while achieving an unobstructed view. Because the vertical pane swings outward, the window shouldn't be installed in a high-traffic area—for example, where the pool guy can walk into it with his pole. Casement windows can be stacked vertically or horizontally to create different design possibilities. They are especially practical in kitchens and bathrooms, although the cam lock on the casement window may be out of reach if the window is placed over a kitchen sink.

PICTURE PERFECT

Picture windows

Picture windows bring light and elegance into any room. They come in all shapes and sizes, including squares, rectangles, circles, trapezoids, octagons, triangles, circle-tops, ellipses and more. To allow for ventilation or egress, the picture window can be combined with any other window styles.

Bay windows

Bay windows are fun. They are especially nice as kitchen and garden windows. There are some considerations to think about before installing one, however. If you don't have a roof overhang above where you want to install the bay window, the window will need to have its own roof built onto it. Bay windows must also be supported from below.

These windows are available in different angles. The 45-degree angle creates the most depth. Within a bay window, you can add casements, awnings or jalousies. An all-glass bay window offers an unobstructed view—each pane of glass is sealed to the adjacent panes, with no frames involved.

Bay windows extend be-yond the exterior wall, creating the illusion of additional space.

Bow windows

If you want a window seat for your house, the bow window has a gentle curve to it. The more units you have, the larger the area for a window seat. An all-casement bow window is a good choice.

TACKLING WATER SPOTS ON WINDOWS

WINDOWS ON THE WATER-FRONT TAKE A SERIOUS BEATING FROM SEA SPRAY AND SALT AIR, QUICKLY BUILDING UP FILM AND WATER SPOTS. YOU CAN HAVE THE GLASS TREATED WITH A PRODUCT CALLED HYDROSHIELD, WHICH CAN ONLY BE APPLIED BY A PROFESSIONAL. WITH PROP-ER MAINTENANCE, THE PROD-UCT WILL KEEP YOUR WINDOWS CLEAR AND CLEAN. TO FIND A DEALER IN HAWAII, GO TO <WWW.HYDROSHIELD.NET>

Cabinets

Selecting the right cabinetry for your kitchen or bath takes on special significance in Hawaii, where salt air, humidity and wet climate zones will affect the longevity and performance of the wood and hardware.

From style, construction and durability to ease of cleaning and the types of wood used—when it comes to choosing cabinets, it pays to know what goes on behind closed doors.

INTO THE WOODS

Because cabinets won't last forever in Hawaii, it's not uncommon to have to replace them within 15 years if you live in a wet and rainy area. And if you have those cheap, pre-fabricated cabinets, don't be surprised if you end up with warped doors, sagging shelves, rotting wood and peeling veneer in a few short years.

Custom cabinetry, on the other hand, will add value to your home. When it comes time to sell your house or have it appraised, instead of the word "average" written in the column listing the appraiser's valuation of your prefab production cabinets, the word "custom" will yield a higher overall value for your home, not to mention a happier homeowner. Sure, custom cabinets are more expensive than prefab, but there is no comparison when it comes to beauty, functionality and value.

Aesthetics and trends aside, the hardwoods typically used in cabinet construction on the mainland will work in Hawaii. Woods that hold up well in humidity include cherry, oak, Lyptus® (a Brazilian hybrid hardwood), maple, alder and hickory. Although light oak might be considered passé in terms of design appeal, Lyptus in particular can exude a certain tropical look.

With veneer technology, an exotic wood like koa, wenge or monkeypod can be applied in a micro-thin sheet over medium-density fiberboard, making pricier woods suddenly more affordable. The rising trend in veneer cabinetry has taken Hawaii's high-end home market by storm, allowing residents to experiment with all sorts of tropical hardwood designs while reducing the ecological impact on rare resources like koa.

Regardless of the type of wood used, wood cabinets are, in actuality, furniture, and should be cleaned with furniture cleaner, not soap and water.

Custom cabinetry lasts longer than pre-fabricated cabinets and provide added value to your home.

THE GREAT DEBATE: PLYWOOD OR PARTICLEBOARD?

Technically, a cabinet is a box. The quality of a cabinet begins with the construction of the box, not just the type of wood utilized for the door. Plywood and particleboard are the two materials used successfully in the majority of cabinets.

Particleboard gets a bad rap for cabinets, but the truth is, the quality of particleboard depends on the grade.

Cheap particleboard found in pre-fab and home-center cabinets is an entirely different product than the heavy, dense, high-quality material used in high-end cabinet making. Cheap particleboard will expand and warp when wet, not exactly a feature you

Thermofoil is a clear plastic laminate bonded to the cabinet's surface for a slick, easy-to-clean finish.

want in your kitchen and bathrooms. Shelves made from it will sag from the weight of the items stored.

Furniture-grade particleboard is a whole other story. It is often the material of choice for custom cabinets. Cabinetmakers recommend a size that is 3⁄4 of an inch thick, finished on both sides with melamine, a low-pressure laminate. The melamine surface is stable, durable, protective and easy to clean, making it ideal for a cabinet's interior.

Plywood is not necessarily stronger or better than particleboard, but because of consumer perception, many high-end custom cabinetmakers construct all-plywood cabinet boxes.

Furniture-grade plywood is about 20 percent more expensive than particleboard but is lighter and easier to work with. Plywood shelves, if installed properly and sealed with a melamine, can withstand pressure and dampness and will hold up indefinitely. However, plywood varies in thickness almost up to 1/16 of an inch, which sometimes makes it more difficult to construct a perfectly squared cabinet box with doors that are aligned and shelves that are flush.

CABINET STYLES

Unless you live in a perfect, climate-controlled environment where there is little deviation in temperature, you'll want to avoid cabinets constructed with mitered seams at the corner of the door faces. The mitered joint does not do well in Hawaii's humid environment and will literally come apart at the seams.

Solid, raised-panel pieces can also be potentially problematic if not constructed properly as "floating panel" systems, without glue. This prevents checking and splits in the wood due to shrinking and swelling.

When deciding which cabinet style is most suited to your kitchen, consider what your maintenance threshold will be. Raised panels have detailed nooks and crannies that can get caked with dust and dirt. For easy cleaning, families with young children prefer the low-maintenance flat panel with a laminate veneer, which is more durable than a wood veneer. Many residents also like the flat panel because it was the predominant style in most of Hawaii's older homes.

Contemporary, European-style cabinets are defined as "frameless" because the entire front face of the cabinet is covered with a full overlay. In extremely wet areas of Hawaii, this type of cabinet can be less giving if it expands.

Thermofoil is a clear plastic laminate bonded to the wood's surface for a slick, easy-to-clean finish. It does not work well close to high heat, however, because it will peel, especially when located next to a range or above the hood. Although pricey, the lacquer type of Thermofoil is the most durable, can sustain a lot more heat and is easy to maintain. And it's available in beautiful custom colors.

Cabinets made especially for outdoor kitchens and barbecue areas are best made of teak. Any other type of wood used for outdoor cabinets should be finished with Sikkens.

COLORS

In general, Hawaii doesn't follow the trends of the mainland when it comes to color. Tastes are individualistic, although lighter colors for kitchens seem to take precedence. A light wood will make your kitchen look larger and also seems to convey a tropical feeling.

INSPECT YOUR DRAWERS

Drawers constructed of solid wood and dovetail joints are the best bet in Hawaii. A dovetail joint is made so the tails of one side interlock with the pins of the other, creating an inseparable connection. Other methods of joining drawers together include dowels or tongue-and-groove construction. Solid-wood drawers with dovetail joints are definitely stronger than the particleboard drawers with stapled joints found on low-end cabinets.

Whether it's hinges or glides, stainless steel hardware is always the best way to go. Drawer glides mounted beneath the unit increase the width and storage capacity of the drawer by an inch. A full extension will give you full access to the drawer.

BATHROOM CABINETS IN HAWAII

Believe it or not, bathroom cabinets are less likely to swell and shrink in Hawaii than on the mainland. That's because Hawaii bathrooms generally have more airflow coming in from the open screens, allowing hot steam to escape, unlike a mainland bathroom that's all sealed up. Additionally, Hawaii homeowners don't have to heat a home during cold winter months, which will dry out the wood in a sealed bathroom.

Thermofoil finishes are very popular for bathrooms, especially in white. The possibility of heat damage to bathroom Thermofoil is less a factor than it is in a kitchen. ❖

This bathroom cabinetry was finished in matte black rather than a glossy polish. The distinguished-looking gold hardware matches the gold sink that rests in a black granite countertop.

Outdoor Living

Hawaiian Rock Walls

ROCK OF AGES

In old Hawaii, for centuries dry-stack rock walls were built without mortar—constructed for land boundaries, sea walls, cattle barriers, house foundations and, most importantly, heiau.

Some of the most enduring structures on the Islands were built in the dry-stack method. One example is the Mookini Heiau, built in 480 A.D. on the cliffs of North Kohala. Another is the Great Wall at Puuhonua O Honaunau, the ancient sanctuary in South Kona that protected kapu-breakers and the bones of chiefs.

Located on the Big Island's Kohala Coast, the massive Puukohola Heiau is probably the most significant rock structure in Hawaii, built by Kamehameha I in 1790 to ensure his destiny as ruler of all the Islands.

Although your rock wall will likely never become a structure of historic significance, there's nothing else in the world of masonry more decidedly tropical than the Hawaiian rock wall—organic, handsome and brimming with mana.

ROCK STARS: HIRING THE RIGHT MASON

Rock-wall building is an art and talent that requires a good eye. As with other local artisans, the most reputable masons are known primarily through word of mouth. The good ones have been doing it for a long time and understand the mechanical and engineering aspects of building walls.

Although the dry-stack method is still in use today, most rock walls are built with cement and a type of rock called "blue rock," which is easily mined and has a smooth finish.

Before you hire a mason, find out about his reputation from previous clients and take a look at his work. Use a screwdriver to scratch the cement. If it comes apart, he may have skimped on materials. A good mason can set 80 to 100 square feet of wall per day, creating a wall that will withstand the test of time and last for generations.

Masons purchase rock from landowners, obtain rock from quarries or "pick" the rock themselves. The look of rock can differ

Opposite: A superior rock wall fits tightly together like pieces of a puzzle. The entire expanse of this wall features a flat smooth face as well as a smooth cap that is even and flush across the top. Above: A rock wall can function as a retaining wall, planter or decorative element in the garden.

This lava rock wall, showcased at the entry of the house, brings balance to the post-modern feel of the interior. Other choices for interiors include veneers made of pahoehoe lava for a swirling, textured effect.

from island to island.

With its active volcanoes, the Big Island of Hawaii is not just a hot spot for live lava; it's a hotbed of endless miles of lava rock. Consequently, the Big Island is the undisputed capital of rock-wall building in the state.

CONSTRUCTION METHODS

Hawaiian rocks are used to build everything from walls, archways, pillars and fence posts to outdoor showers, mailbox stands and entryways.

Whether it's the mortar or the dry-stack method, the technique for building rock walls is the same. The mason looks for the nicest face and uses a hammer, chisel or chipping gun to piece the rocks together. Each layer is locked into place like a puzzle and set nice and tight.

In general, one layer is locked together by the layer beneath it, with a slight tilt inward for gravity-resistant stability. The interior of the wall is filled with "rubbish rock" hidden inside the hollow of the structure. The correct mixture of cement is a critical element in rock-wall building and is often a family secret among masons.

The superior rock wall fits together perfectly and has a smooth, even face along the expanse of the wall. Sometimes walls might have pipes installed at the base for drainage.

When topping a wall, two basic styles are featured—the rock cap or the cement cap. A rock cap should maintain an even, flat surface and not be made of scattered, jagged rock strewn haphazardly on top of the wall, otherwise known as a lei.

Cement caps are generally less expensive than rock caps and can be designed in a cantilever style, forming a bench with edges that extend over either side. You can put bamboo fencing on top of a rock wall with a cement cap.

TYPES OF ROCK USED IN HAWAIIAN MASONRY

Although blue rock is the most commonly used and least expensive rock in Hawaiian masonry, rock structures can also be made of lava rock—either the rough and jagged a'a or the smooth and ropy pahoehoe.

Moss rock is considered the most desirable choice. As the name suggests, moss rock is covered with bits of green lichen growing on the surface and needs moisture to retain its appearance.

On the Big Island's Kohala Coast, a'a lava is a rugged alternative and is being widely used at resorts. The a'a is abundant and is easy to piece together, say Big Island masons.

Pahoehoe is ideal for veneer, retaining walls, privacy walls and outdoor showers. It's mostly only available on the Big Island. You can get faux pahoehoe cast in cement that looks like the real thing, though. The same is true for moss rock and any other type of rock, for that matter.

Natural pahoehoe is mined in sheets or layers two to three inches thick. A circular saw with a diamond tip is needed to cut or shave the rock. It's then pieced together to achieve a tight, uniform fit.

Before placing veneer, the mason shoots anchors into the wall with a gun and a .22 shell to support the cement. For consistency in color and texture, all the pahoehoe should ideally come from the same site.

The rugged and jagged a'a lava is widely used at Big Island resorts and home sites all across Kona. The look is decidedly different from traditional blue rock found throughout the Islands. Below: Pahoehoe is mined from lava flows in sheets two to three inches thick. It is used primarily for veneer, as featured on this stunning pahoehoe rock wall in Kealakekua Bay.

Lanais

Outdoor entertaining can be elegant when a lanai functions as an indoor-outdoor space, complete with all the accoutrements including a flat-screen TV. Golden Ray quartzite sets the stage in natural stone.

Elsewhere it's called a patio, balcony, porch or veranda. Here in Hawaii, it's the beloved lanai.

For residents and visitors alike, the lanai is as important as the interior living space. Because Hawaii's year-round idyllic climate allows for night and day comfort, the lanai is truly a functional living area that also happens to be outdoors.

SIZE MATTERS

When designing a new home, it's important to consider how your lanai area will affect the lot coverage allowed by your home-owners' association. Whether it's a ground-floor patio or a wood balcony off a second story, a lanai might be counted as part of the total square footage of a home, particularly at a high-end resort development. If you have 40-percent lot coverage, for example, that dimension could be measured to include the outside walls or columns whether the area is enclosed or not.

The size of your lanai depends on your budget, but six feet out from the wall is the absolute minimum that will accommo-date two chairs and a table, like at a condo. Conversely, the ideal lanai is as spacious as possible, with plenty of room to spread out and relax and also have enough space for all those important accoutrements, like patio furniture, an umbrella, chaises longues, dog beds, tiki bars, beer kegs and so forth. If you want to put heavy appliances such as a portable spa, weight machines or a heavy-duty barbecue system on a bal-cony lanai, be sure to confer with a structural engineer.

With a density that's twice as hard as most other hardwoods, ipe is ideal for high-traffic areas such as front door steps and lanai.

For safety reasons, 36 inches is the minimum height for a rail-ing on an upper-level lanai. In actuality, 39 inches is preferable, because it's above the hip level of an average adult, a precaution that might come in handy for that occasional reeling guest who's had one too many. There should also be no more than four inch-es of space between each picket so that no child can fall through. Consult your local Uniform Building Code to confirm.

To ensure proper drainage, a lanai should be constructed at least half an inch below the level of the interior finish area. This is one of several steps architects take to keep water from com-ing into the house. Another is to waterproof the break between the two areas with copper or aluminum flashing or a waterproof membrane.

AS ABOVE, SO BELOW

Because of Hawaii's searing sun and frequent rains, it's best to have an overhang above your lanai with at least 30-percent coverage so there is an area to retreat to when those afternoon showers come or when the sun is at its most intense. For full

Seamless glass railings offer an obstructed view when you are sitting on a lanai such as this one overlooking a pebble beach in South Kona. Retrofitting an existing railing with glass is quick and relatively easy.

coverage, an overhang should encompass the area of the lanai or patio plus another three to five feet beyond—that way you can sit outside during inclement weather as well as on beautiful, sunny-sky days.

In Hawaii, lanais are usually built on the ocean side of the house. On the north side of a house, they are subject to more wind and rain, as trade winds come from the northeast.

If you want to build a leak-proof lanai above a patio or room, it needs to be fully enclosed and have some type of drainage system in place. A lanai made of cement usually has tile or stone installed over a waterproof membrane on a cement float. An open-slatted wood deck, on the other hand, will not keep the occasional spilt drink from leaking through the slats and dripping on the occupants below.

A new polyvinyl product with a built-in gutter is just starting to be used in lanai construction in Hawaii. It features interlocking vinyl decking material that spans across the joists to create a waterproof environment. Water falls into a groove and travels across the deck and out.

Don't forget to plan for your water and electrical needs when you're designing. If you want to be able to water potted plants or fill a spa, you'll need to have a spigot in close proximity. To eliminate the need for outside wiring, solar lighting is an option.

RAILINGS

Wood pickets and steps are the first components of a lanai that will start to show sign of deterioration from the elements. Wood rails should be put together with stainless-steel screws so that they don't rust out and fall apart. The pickets should be designed so that they don't capture and hold water where they meet the bottom rail. The ideal wood railing is constructed with a camber or cant, so that there's a slight pitch for shedding water.

Pre-made aluminum rail systems are a cost-effective option over wood, but there is quite an aesthetic trade-off.

Glass railings have become a part of contemporary Island-style architecture. Framed glass is less expensive than a seamless design, which would be the ideal installation for an unobstructed view. If you want to retrofit an existing lanai with a glass railing, you don't have to rip the railing apart to do it. Just remove the pickets, put in the stops and wood trim, and you're good to go.

SCREEN STARS AND OTHER SHADY CHARACTERS

Because of bugs and mosquitoes, some residents prefer to screen in their entire lanais, creating a sort of Florida-style living environment. This is a matter of personal preference. Screens will keep the bugs out, but at the expense of ventilation. An alternative solution is to install retractable screens, either manual or motorized, that can cover the expanse of the lanai from top beam to bottom of the railings.

The afternoon sun can be brutal when you're sitting outside, but there are all sorts of options for shades and awnings. Solar shades can cut out 95 percent of the sunlight while maintaining visibility. A retractable awning can provide vast areas of shade, up to 480 feet.

SOME FINISHING TOUCHES

Protecting a wood deck from the elements is a constant battle. If the sun and rain weren't enough, objects like potted plants that sit on the lanai and won't allow the wood underneath to breathe can cause mold, rot and deterioration over time. Inspect beneath those potted plants to make sure this isn't happening.

For wood lanais, exterior paint is the best option—it will offer the most protection against the elements, especially in wet elevations. If you're planning on staining your deck, use Sikkens, a marine-grade product that holds up the best. To protect exposed wood, some people opt to apply layers of oil.

Ipe is an up-and-coming hardwood that is finding success for use as decking material. It can be left natural as long as it's put together with stainless-steel screws and biscuits, which are pre-made plastic clamps that prevent warping and movement. Trex® decking and railing products are made from composite wood and plastic that won't rot or splinter and will still retain a natural wood look.

Landscaping Basics

To maximize space in a small yard, keep things clean and classic using only about a half dozen different varieties of plants. Simple lines keep the look of your yard clutter free.

Whether you're a kamaaina or a newcomer to the Islands, planning your landscaping takes some research. With its many microclimates, Hawaii presents a variety of environments suited to specific plants. Choosing the right plants and right place to plant them will reduce your maintenance efforts and increase the joy of tropical gardening. Understanding what grows best at your elevation is key to success.

RIGHT PLANT, RIGHT PLACE, NO PROBLEM . . .

Do you live mauka or makai? Your elevation affects all sorts of gardening conditions, such as temperature range, average rainfall, soil type, amount of salt in the air and amount of sun you receive. Each of these conditions should influence what type of plants you select and how you will need to water and maintain them.

Some plants are not salt tolerant and won't do well at lower elevations. Noni and plumeria are at home at sea level but won't thrive in upper elevations. Standard gardenias and ixora are acid-loving plants that don't like the more alkaline soil found at lower elevations. Drought-resistant groundcovers like naio papa, wedelia and ilima papa are ideally suited for low or windy locales and slopes.

Pink acalypha can inject color and contrast into monochromatic landscaping.

In your eagerness to fill your open space with plants, remember that over-planting can be a crucial mistake in Hawaii—your yard could become an unmanageable jungle! That cute little potted plant you installed today could become a massive 15-foot tree in a matter of a few years. Additionally, planting trees and bushes too close to your pool, spa or pond can produce a maintenance headache you'll soon regret.

When deciding where to plant trees, factor in the direction of the trade winds as well as the need for shade trees on the south- and west-facing sides where the sun is the hottest.

Bare soil without the protection of plants or mulch can erode and will likely attract the weeds that grow in the tropics year round. Mulch is an absolute necessity in Hawaii: it keeps the soil alive with all those tiny organisms it needs to thrive. Wood chips, compost and macadamia nut husks all make good mulch.

Whether you use the soil you already have or purchase amended soils, you can get your soil tested by your local extension office. The test measures the acidity and nutrient levels and will you help you determine ways to increase your soil's fertility.

Plants in Hawaii might grow slightly slower in winter months, but most have a very short dormant period. This can only mean one thing: year-round maintenance and weeding! The best defense against weeds and pests? Healthy, established plants...and soil that's planted or mulched.

GOING NATIVE WITH NATIVE PLANTS

Native plants thrive in Hawaii for a reason—they've been

Maintaining an in-ground pond requires a gardener's mentality. If you like gardening, then you'll probably do well with a pond as part of your landscaping.

here for centuries and are well adapted to the climate and weather patterns.

The best way to decide which plants are right for your yard is to view them in their natural settings. Visit your local botanical gardens to learn more about native species and to see mature example of plants you might want to use, as well as to observe xeriscape (dry-area planting) fundamentals in action. The use of drought-tolerant and low-maintenance plants will greatly enhance your gardening experience.

Native plants used ornamentally include the shrub ilima, as well as naio papa and ilima papa, which are groundcovers. Loulu is a native fan palm. A small native tree called alahee makes a nice living Christmas tree.

One of the only fragrant hibiscuses in the world is the native kokio keokeo. There's also an attractive native Hawaiian gardenia known as nanu. The beautiful and exotic hala tree brings an aura of tropical elegance to lower elevation locales. And noni, the so-called "famine fruit" tree that thrives at sea level, is nearly indestructible. The famous koa tree is indigenous to the upland forests, but you can enjoy its smaller relative, the koaie, at lower elevations.

When you begin to discover native plants and their significance to Hawaiian culture, it will bring a whole new dimension to your horticultural pursuits.

WATERING AND IRRIGATION

If you live below 800 feet in elevation, you'll need an irrigation plan. Whether you choose to water your yard yourself or install an irrigation system, planting drought-tolerant plants is a smart move.

On the other hand, one of the most common gardening mistakes in Hawaii is over-watering, so don't go to the extreme of loving your plants to death with too much water. Plants are healthier when they are watered deeply but less frequently. Ideally, watering two to three times a week for 20 minutes is a good rule of thumb. Daily watering causes shallow root growth and overdependence on your daily dose, and can lead to plant diseases and pest problems. Less frequent watering will help your plants develop the moisture reserves they need to carry them through hot, dry periods.

The best time to water your yard is just before sunrise, which keeps the water from evaporating quickly and also prevents the

sun from burning the wet foliage (each water droplet acts like a magnifying glass). If you run your irrigation system after sunset, you could be attracting slugs and snails that will eat your plants.

When the rainy season comes, you'll want to make some adjustments in your normal watering routine. If it's raining every day or even every other day, turn off your irrigation system for the duration.

Top from left to right: Croton, gardenia, monsterra, desert rose. **Bottom from left to right:** sagittaria water plant, agapanthus, plumeria, gardenia.

A LITTLE PRIVACY, PLEASE

Is your neighbor breathing down your neck, literally? Foliage and trees offer ideal privacy screens and also create some sound-proofing, helping to keep your neighbor's activities out of sight and out of mind. And because most plants grow really fast in Hawaii, you won't have to wait for years until your foliage is tall enough to become an effective screen.

Good screens can be achieved with panax, podocarpus, areca palm, some varieties of bamboo and, at lower elevations, sea grape. All grow fast and remain bushy from top to bottom. Although poisonous if eaten, oleander and its relative "bee-still" also do a nice job of keeping distance between you and your neighbors. Hau is a native tree that grows tall and can be pruned to remain bushy. If you go with bamboo, plant only the clumping kind, not the running. Hibiscus will also provide thick foliage—there are several varieties that are resistant to the destructive mites that frequently infest them.

Container gardening is a good choice for small backyards and to enhance outdoor living spaces. Containers of potted plants add life and color to this ornamental rock garden.

FOR SMALL BACKYARDS, TRY CONTAINER GARDENING

If you have a small backyard or a large lanai, container gardening is the way to go. Pots, urns and vessels of various shapes and sizes, as well as the plants themselves, can bring a decorative element to your outdoor living space. Bamboos and palms are excellent choices for plants in containers. Citrus trees will thrive, as well as vegetables such as tomatoes and peppers. Ubiquitous in Hawaii landscape design are crotons—hardy, tropical plants that are very sun tolerant. There are many varieties of crotons with colorful foliage that ranges from reds, oranges and yellows to green, and some have multi-colored spots and variegation. All of the croton varieties can be used as attractive container plants.

IT PAYS TO PLAN AHEAD

If you're building a new home, you might want to set aside a landscaping budget in advance. Hiring a professional to help with landscape design can save you money in the long run. You could also consult a designer on an hourly basis to address many of your concerns.

Do hire a professional to install irrigation. It takes expertise to determine proper placement, the gallons-per-minute requirement of your plants, and all the things necessary to keep your water bill minimal and your plants' health optimal.

When it comes to plant selection, survey your neighborhood to find out what is thriving. What works on the mainland doesn't necessarily work in the Islands. If you are going to do your own landscaping, it's important not to go willy-nilly with just any kind of plants. Take a class, buy a book and do some research. Your local outdoor circle may offer master gardener programs and basic courses in landscaping, native plants, xeriscape, irrigation and more. For information on classes offered by local landscaping associations, the Landscape Industry Council of Hawaii, a statewide landscaping organization, is a good resource. (licHawaii.com).

With a little foresight and some imagination, your landscaping will greatly enhance the overall impact, pleasure and value of your new home.

Outdoor Lighting

Go Lite on Lighting:
A dramatic outdoor
setting can be achieved
with a few low-voltage
lights, some candles and
a nicely lit pond.

Your tropical landscaping looks great in the daytime, but with the right kind of lighting, it can be downright stunning at night. Illuminating your garden with outdoor lighting creates magical and dramatic effects, at the same time making your property more secure and your paths, steps and walkways safer for walking.

GETTING A FIX ON FIXTURES

Outdoor light fixtures in Hawaii must be strong enough to withstand the demanding tropical environment. When it comes to fixtures, the three most corrosion-resistant materials are copper, brass and aluminum. Solid brass makes an excellent, non-corrosive fixture. Although it may darken in color over time, with a coated finish it will hardly fade at all. Coated copper fixtures come in a variety of different finishes and will generally keep their color. Like brass, copper won't rust, but it will often patina into a desirable look. Some copper fixtures have a patina finish that's applied at the factory.

Powder-coated aluminum fixtures will last longer than stainless steel, but may start to pit, especially on the underside, nearest the ground. Plastic fixtures are usually made with a UV-blocking agent, but not all plastics are created equal. Higher-end plastic fixtures are manufactured with composite materials like Trisyn®.

When shopping for an outdoor fixture, make sure it has a wet or damp rating. A wet rating means the material can come in direct contact with water like rain or sprinklers. Damp-rated fixtures can handle some moisture and are best located in an area that's protected by a roof overhang.

The quality of the fixture is not simply dictated by the materials used. The fixture should be able to retain a tight seal after you've changed out the bulb, and the screws should remain intact.

BULBS—DIM AND OTHERWISE

In the world of outdoor lighting, bulbs are known as "lamps." Although they are more expensive, florescent lamps have a longer life than standard bulbs and are much more energy efficient. A so-called "bug light" has a yellow hue that's not as attractive to insects (and some humans), but unfortunately it won't keep bugs away entirely.

Low-voltage halogen bulbs cast a crisp light with twice the brightness of a regular light bulb. Many pathway lights utilize the low-watt halogen because the tiny bulb is the ideal size for the amount of light it emits.

Fiberoptics is a new technology in which thin strands of glass are encased in a plastic tube though which the light is emitted. A wheel of colors travels through the optical cable for varying light patterns.

A motion sensor light turns on when it detects movement, which can be annoying if it's right outside your bedroom window. The better-quality motion sensor lights have different settings so they don't turn on when a dog or cat passes by.

In the category of "dim bulb," solar lights have a long way to go, but improved technology could be around the corner. In the meantime, solar garden lights, while energy efficient, offer little more than a faint glow in the darkness.

LOW-VOLTAGE LANDSCAPE LIGHTING

These days, most landscape lighting is done with low-voltage systems that use a 12-volt current. Not only are these systems energy efficient, they are safe, easy to install and provide a much longer lamp life than 120-volt fixtures, which are also larger and more obtrusive. Once installed, low-voltage lights can be expanded or repositioned with ease, even with the power on—which is especially helpful when you're positioning and rearranging your lights at night.

Outdoor fixtures should be made of corrosion-resistant materials, either brass, copper or aluminum. Like brass, copper won't rust, but will often patina into a desirable look.

With low-voltage lighting, you don't have to run the cable in a deep trench either. Just dig a light trench 3 to 4 inches deep and cover the cable with cinder. You can even run the cable up the side of a tree if necessary. Just make sure your cables and fixtures can't be mowed down by gardening equipment or knocked down by people or dogs passing through.

Low-voltage systems include a transformer, lights and cables. The transformer reduces household current to 12 volts and controls the amount of time that the lights are on. Just plug it into your exterior outlet. Most transformers feature a timer that can be set for four, six or eight hours. Some have a photocell that turns the lights on when it gets dark and then off in the daytime, but because with this option your lights will be on all night, most people prefer an on-off switch or a timer.

The size of the transformer depends on how many lights you have. If you have 40 fixtures each using a 10-watt bulb, for example, you would need a 400-watt transformer. Additionally, make sure the transformer housings are corrosion resistant.

You can purchase an all-inclusive 12-volt lighting set from

The right amount of lighting can add an attractive visual effect to your outdoor haven. The use of exotic plant species enhances the tropical look.

your local hardware store or big-box retailer, but the 12-volt architectural-grade systems will give you more options, a range of different wattage and superior quality than standard kits. In other words, you get what you pay for.

Voltage drop is a potential occurrence with any low-voltage system. Fixtures at the end of the line, those farthest from the transformer, are especially susceptible to dimming. Using heavy-gauge direct-burial cable like a #10 or #8 can help. You can also try splitting the line at the midpoint and going back toward the transformer with one of the lines. A multi-volt transformer will help compensate for voltage drops on long cable runs.

TRIPPING THE LIGHT FANTASTIC

If landscape lighting is an art, then your yard is the canvas. Professional lighting designers know how to create subtle moods and understated effects by balancing levels of brightness and highlighting a few focal points. The artful use of ground-mounted and overhead light sources is the secret to success.

With outdoor lighting, a garden is generally divided into three zones. The foreground retains a mid-level brightness, while the middle grounds feature intriguing shadows and low-level light. To draw the eye through the garden, the background is often the brightest of the three zones. Streetlights and other competing sources of light must be taken into consideration.

HOW TO UPLIGHT A COCONUT TREE

Depending on the height of the tree, you can begin with less wattage, anywhere from 10 to 50 watts, and as the tree gets taller change the wattage and beam spread. Low-voltage lighting provides excellent light source for coconut trees. For uplighting, there are several options of lamps to try, so consult with your lighting specialist. An in-ground mounted light with a grate will protect the lamp from traffic, falling coconuts and other hazards.

Plumeria and hala can also be uplighted anywhere between 20 and 50 watts depending on how big the tree is. The beam spread will usually range from 20 to 60 degrees.

Low-voltage lighting will actually provide enough light and beam spread to uplight a coconut tree. Try installing an in-ground light that will be protected from falling coconuts and other potential hazards.

MORE LIGHTING TIPS

• FOR WALKWAYS, ALTERNATE EDGE LIGHTS IN A ZIGZAG PATTERN INSTEAD OF LINING EACH SIDE OF THE PATH LIKE AN AIRPORT RUNWAY. LIGHTS CAN BE POSITIONED AT LEAST SIX FEET APART FOR THE DESIRED EFFECT.

• CREATE A CONTRASTING PALETTE OF LIGHT AND DARK INSTEAD OF ILLUMINATING AN ENTIRE AREA LIKE A PARKING LOT.

• MULTIPLE LIGHT SOURCES GIVE AN OBJECT DIMENSION, WHILE A SINGLE, DIRECT LIGHT SOURCE WILL MAKE IT LOOK FLATTER.

• BE AWARE OF HOW YOUR LIGHTING WILL AFFECT YOUR NEIGHBORS. MAKE SURE YOU ARE IN COMPLIANCE WITH YOUR NEIGHBORHOOD'S CC&RS (COVENANTS, CODES AND RESTRICTIONS).

• LIGHTING THE SURF FROM AN OCEANFRONT HOME COULD BE A VIOLATION OF LOCAL CODES— PLUS, IT IS THOUGHT TO IMPACT TURTLES AND OTHER MARINE LIFE ADVERSELY.

• DIRECTIONAL LIGHTING INVOLVES UPLIGHTING A TREE OR OBJECT TO CREATE A BEAUTIFUL AND DRAMATIC LOOK. DOWNLIGHTING FROM TREES OR STRUCTURES WILL GENTLY WASH THE AREA BELOW WITH NATURAL ACCENTS.

Ponds

This pond features plant "sleeves," containers in which potted plants can be easily inserted and rotated. The result is a landscape that always looks as if it is in bloom.

Ahhh…The soothing sounds of a beautiful waterfall trickling over moss-laden lava rock into a tranquil pond brimming with colorful koi fish and exotic water lilies.

Sound romantic? Yes, until the cruel realties of maintaining this complex ecosystem become as loud and clear as the roaring mating call of the giant toad that's now a permanent resident in your backyard.

Maintaining a pond in Hawaii is a challenge, but if you're aware of the pros and cons before embarking on the project, you could be on your way to discovering a lifelong hobby that will bring you joy for years to come.

GETTING CLEAR ABOUT PONDS

In Hawaii, a beautiful pond often serves as an architectural feature of the home, whether for entryways, atriums or patios. In a backyard, a pond adds interest to the landscaping. If you want to go simple, a tabletop pond for your lanai might be just the solution. Ponds can be made any number of ways, with containers, urns, tubs or troughs.

Building an authentic, in-ground pond requires an artful touch and a gardener's mentality. If you like gardening, then you'll probably do well with a pond. If you're not up for the task, you might end up like hundreds of other frustrated pond owners and decide to turn your pond into a planter when the inevitable "pond fatigue" syndrome sets in.

COSTS

There are a few basic truths that should be considered before diving into pond ownership. First and foremost, it costs money to run a pond. The bigger the pond, the more money it takes to run the pump and filter. Buying the right equipment up front will make the difference.

Smaller plants near a pond are preferable to large, fruit-bearing trees that have aggressive roots and drop lots of debris into the water. For an absolutely clear-water pond, avoid the use of fish or plants and add a little bleach every so often to keep it algae free.

Don't go cheap with a $60 pump. It could end up costing you $75 a month just to run it. Compare that to the $12 a month in electricity you'll spend on a $350 pump, and you'll see why a cheap pump is simply a waste of money. Plus, a cheap pump won't last for more than a couple of months, and it won't do the job of moving the water.

Conversely, avoid using pool equipment for ponds. A pool filter is not designed for a pond and will be too expensive to run.

There are two types of pumps. Submersible pumps are quiet and need no entry hole into the pond, but they do tend to make the water warmer. An "outside" pump makes a little more noise and needs an entry hole, but it is easier to maintain.

Filters make the water clear. They require additional maintenance as well as a pump in order to run. If you go the bio-filter route, you'll need to run it 24 hours a day, which will add to your electric bill. With a bio-filter, you'll also want to have a spare pump and filter on hand in the event your bio-filter breaks down, in which case the water could become toxic within 12 hours.

If your pond is more than 24 inches deep, it will need to comply with county regulations for swimming pools. A pond this size should also be listed on your homeowners' insurance policy.

Koi ponds are a stunning addition to entryways. Keep in mind when you stock your pond that koi fish will grow bigger and may overtake the size of the pond.

Keep in mind that you'll have a difficult—if not impossible—time finding a pond technician or gardener who will come out for weekly maintenance. A majority of pool-cleaning services will refuse to service a pond. What's more, once-a-week maintenance may not be sufficient to keep your pond in working order. A pond with fish in it is something that should be observed and monitored daily.

These are all good reasons why to be a successful water garden enthusiast in Hawaii, you must be passionate about your hobby.

PLANTS AND FISH

Will your pond attract mosquitoes? Not if you have fish! The great thing about fish is that they keep the mosquitoes away. Mosquito larvae are like popcorn to a fish. Some pond owners actually grow mosquitoes to feed their fish.

The bigger the fish, the bigger their needs. Koi are the top-of-the-line pond fish and have the most requirements. If you go on vacation, you'll want to hire a fish sitter to keep an eye on your valuable koi, which if cared for properly can live for 200 years.

Large fish loads require a pump that runs 24 hours a day. Don't make the mistake of turning your pump off at night—the pond's level of oxygen is at its lowest between midnight and 6 a.m. Overfeeding of fish is another common mistake. Fish will live longer if you feed them less.

Plants or no plants? This is a good question. The truth is, it is nearly impossible to have big fish, plants *and* clear water all in the same pond. If you're going to grow plants like water lilies or water hyacinths, they need 60-percent sun, but they will also produce algae.

To counter this, cover 60 percent of your pond with plants and keep them corralled at one end of the pond with fishing line, keeping the rest of the pond clear for the fish. A pond will balance itself with the right fish load, the right kind of plants and proper amount of shade. Slime water can be added to a new pond to speed the balancing process.

You can create a pond with a small fish load and water hyacinths so long as you keep the larger-growth hyacinths cleared out once a week.

A green pond is not necessarily a bad thing. Chinese ponds, for example, are kept green because the algae offers a mirror-like reflection off the surface, creating an aesthetic appeal.

If all you want is the sound of running water near your house, a pond with no fish or plants is the way to go. Just add a little bleach once in a while and you're all set.

WATERFALLS AND SPRAYS

A waterfall spilling over natural rock looks great, but will add to your monthly cost in electricity. Additionally, it's difficult to avoid water loss due to evaporation because water tends to seep through the porous rocks and away from the pond. To solve this problem, put the waterfall in the middle of the pond—that way you won't lose as much water to leaching.

Bubble sprays don't work in a pond. They end up getting clogged daily, spurting and sputtering rather than producing that clear, thin umbrella of water over the pond.

MATERIALS AND LOCATION

Your choice of location for the pond is key. The amount of sun, shade, size of the pond and whether you want clear or cloudy water are just some of the determining factors to be considered before undertaking the project. And be sure to build the pond in a place where you can see and enjoy it!

Above-ground ponds can be safer than in-ground ponds if you've got kids around, and they are also easier to maintain. You can siphon debris from the bottom instead of having to drain it, and you don't have to worry about runoff problems during heavy rain.

For surfaces, concrete or gunite (sprayed-on concrete) work best. Flexible liners offer a range of design possibilities, but the edges and sides are sometimes difficult to hide completely.

No matter where you build your pond in Hawaii, you will likely get toads. Toads and pond ownership go hand in hand, so be prepared to add "toad hunting" to your list of pond duties.

Water features provide the soothing sounds of trickling water. If you want to avoid excess evaporation, try placing rock waterfalls in the middle of your pond so that you don't lose water to leaching.

Pool Decks

A backyard oasis begins with a firm foundation—your deck. With the superb range of materials available, you can achieve a stunning outdoor setting with a variety of textures, colors and looks. Combined with tropical landscaping, a first-rate entertainment area and a beautiful swimming pool, the deck is the underlying element that pulls the whole scene together.

Decks surrounding a pool can run the gamut from traditional or decorative concrete to tile, exposed aggregate, composite wood or natural stone. Different materials present specific advantages and limitations, not to mention costs.

The two most important considerations are drainage and heat absorption. Your concrete contractor is responsible for figuring out the best lay of the land for proper drainage. You are the one who has the ultimate say in what decking material will work best for you.

Trex® composite is made of 50-percent wood and 50-percent plastic. It bends and curves, creating appealing deck designs that are not feasible with natural wood.

ON DECK—SELECTING THE RIGHT MATERIAL

Some colors and materials may look fantastic from a distance, but walking barefoot across a dark surface on a hot, sunnyday is an entirely different story. Glazed tile, for example, can heat up fast and turn slick when wet. Red brick and flagstone are other materials that can become too hot to walk on in the Hawaii sun.

While the right material is key to a lasting deck, proper installation makes a huge difference in performance and drainage. With tile or stone, make sure your contractor does not skip the important step of setting an anti-fracture membrane beneath the stone installation. Bonded to the concrete below and the tile above, the membrane prevents cracking caused by the shrinkage or movement of the concrete slab due to heat and other factors. Typically, when failure occurs with exterior stone applications, it's because this crucial element is lacking or has not been installed with the procedure as put forth by national industry guidelines, which too many contractors in Hawaii have been ignoring in recent years. Expansion joints, which allow for contraction and expansion along the grout lines, may also be installed.

Staining, another problem with decks, is most commonly caused by stagnant water. A penetrating sealer is usually applied to protect pool decks. Keep that red cinder gravel away from your pool deck as well—red cinder is notorious for staining cement and stone.

With a protective sealant and proper installation and drainage, your deck should be quite durable, no matter the material selected.

Flamed, bush-hammered granite is usually sold in tiles and cubes for a cobblestone effect. Rougher stones emulate an older, rustic quality.

FOR POOL DECKS, STONE IS A NATURAL

When selecting stone for your pool deck, be sure to let your stone vendor know what you will be using it for so that you can get the best advice possible.

Flamed granite is a new and upscale choice in Hawaii and is being used successfully for facings, stairs and pool copings. Its colors and wavy pattern are produced by exposure to intense heat, creating a deeply textured surface that is slip-resistant when wet. Most granite is quartz-based and traps heat, and therefore it is generally not used for an entire pool deck because it can get hot. For decorative purposes, flamed granite can be combined with polished granite for a dramatic contrast.

Second in hardness to granite is quartzite. It's also considerably less expensive. Quartzite comes in a brushed, rough finish that offers plenty of traction. It's available in an array of colors like grays, yellows, greens and reds for a variety of different looks. To better reflect heat, a lighter-colored quartzite is more practical for a pool deck. With its multi-colored neutral tones, Golden Ray is often used in Hawaii and will complement most of the colors surrounding it.

A calcium-based stone, travertine is twice as expensive as quartzite. While travertine can get slippery when wet, it is a popular choice in Hawaii for pool decks. A brushed, tumbled or antiqued finish will offer the most traction. Homeowners like travertine because they can they can blend their indoor flooring with their outside decking and retain the same visual tone. Because travertine is porous, though, you should seal it approximately once a year.

For pool decks, you'll want to avoid slate, sandstone and darker materials like lava rock. Sandstone, with its natural, slip-resistant texture, is among the new trends in decking on the mainland, but it doesn't perform well in Hawaii. Slate, with its natural flakiness and lack of durability, doesn't work well in Hawaii for pool decks, either. It is also known to produce a reddish stain that could seep into your pool. A good scrub-down is needed no matter where you decide to install it.

If installed properly, stone-look porcelain is an ideal decking material because it is zero maintenance. And you don't even have to seal it. Since it is made to look like stone, it has plenty of traction and is actually ADA-approved for commercial uses. Stones replicated include tumbled travertine, quartzite and slate.

CONCRETE SURFACES

In Hawaii, heat will break down the setting materials underneath any type of stone installation over time. The fact is, a natural stone deck won't last forever.

For pool decks, the most reliable surface continues to be concrete. Stenciled and stamped concrete is a great way to add color, patterns and texture to plain concrete after it has just been poured. The finished look can be that of natural brick or stone with a contrasting grout line. A protective coating will seal and strengthen the concrete, while the surface can be rough-broomed for an anti-slip finish. A coral-mix concrete replicates a sand finish but takes a specialist to achieve the best results.

Spray-on textured-concrete products are applied to existing concrete to create a strong, non-slip surface that is firmly bonded with the slab below. The result is a colored, textured surface that holds up well against the elements.

Regular concrete pool decks should be sealed to prevent cracking, mold, slickness and staining. Some coatings will even lower the surface temperature of the deck.

Smooth stone surfaces are created using a mixture of small river rocks and epoxy resin for a slip-resistant finish. The patented product is installed on the top of existing concrete in a thickness of half an inch. Because the material is porous, water drains away under the concrete. Decorative elements like petroglyphs and borders in contrasting colors can be incorporated.

Quartzite stone is a popular choice in Hawaii for pool decks. Proper installation is key for any natural stone application in order for it to hold up against the elements.

If the idea of installing Astroturf on your pool deck comes to mind, banish it! The mildew factor is only exceeded by the tackiness.

Futura Stone manufactures a type of decking material that transforms the average deck into a masterpiece of creative designs. Honu mosaics are achieved through the use of contrasting-colored river rocks.

WHAT WOULD WOOD DO?

Because of the sun, pool chemicals, continual moisture and lots of foot traffic, it's virtually impossible to achieve long-lasting results around a pool using lumber. But there is an alternative.

Composite woods perform well and are sized to match conventional lumber. Although composites are not strong enough to be used for support structures, they hold up great for flooring and railings.

Some composites are made of recycled plastic and waste-wood, while others, like eon® composite, are made of 100-percent plastic and simulate wood's natural texture and grain without the need for sanding, staining or weatherproofing. eon comes in coastal gray, cedar and redwood colors.

Made of a 50/50 plastic and wood mix, Trex® is flexible enough to curve around a pool, allowing for designs that are not possible with wood. An added benefit of this type of composite is that it can be milled along the edges just like wood. Trex® decking is highly resistant to the damaging effects of UV rays and is available in many different colors.

Although composites are usually more costly than wood, the longevity factor and lack of maintenance will outweigh the cost in the long run.

Pool Maintenance

Tile is the top-of-the line for pool surfaces. Although expensive, tiled surfaces are durable and easy to maintain, as well as highly aesthetic and upscale.

Maintaining a pool in Hawaii is a slightly different proposition than having one on the mainland. Year-round usage requires extra maintenance and cleaning every week to deal with the effects of the tropical elements. What's more, the cost of utilities, equipment and chemicals is much higher in the Islands than elsewhere in the country.

These and other factors should be considered if you are going to successfully maintain an efficient and long-lasting pool. Before you dive into pool ownership, examine your cost expectations versus the realities.

A HEATED DISCUSSION

How and when to heat your pool is a primary consideration. Even on the hottest day, most pools in Hawaii need some kind of heating system. Although temperature is a personal preference, a pool kept at over 85 degrees will be hard to maintain and more expensive to heat.

Solar pool covers

The least expensive option for heating your pool is the solar cover, a blue-plastic "bubble" sheet cut to fit the shape of the pool. Floating on the water's surface, the cover retains heat and can increase water temperature by up to 11 degrees. Not every pool is a candidate for a pool cover, depending on design configurations, and some people might find a pool cover to be downright unattractive.

Additionally, a pool cover needs to be removed every time you want to take a dip. Rather than placing it in a heap on the deck where it will accumulate dirt and leaves, the better option is to purchase a reel system so that the cover can easily be rolled up. The average pool cover will last about two to three years.

Propane

In Hawaii, propane is most commonly used to heat pools. It is far more efficient than electricity because it will heat the water more quickly. There are many gas heaters on the market available in varying price ranges.

Solar

Although pricy, solar heating is one of the best ways to heat a pool. Once the system is installed, it will run itself and save on energy costs.

POOL SURFACES

Along with creating a desired ambiance, certain pool colors can make a difference in water temperature. Black, gray and blue surfaces heat up the water an average of six degrees.

Although they have the look of a natural pond, black pools are generally not recommended. You can't really tell how deep the water is, plus it's difficult to see debris when you're cleaning. Never dive into a black pool!

Blue and black plasters tend to fade over time, while gray

and white hold up over the long haul. A gray pool will actually have a soothing blue hue and is highly recommended. For some people, bright white plaster can be a little *too* bright.

Major mistake #1: don't paint a plaster surface to cover up blemishes and stains. The paint won't last, it will cloud your pool and it will end up costing you more when you finally submit to the fact that you have to re-plaster. Then your old paint will have to be removed first, an extra step that you'll be charged for.

POOL DESIGNS

A simple, rectangular pool is the gold standard for pool design, especially if you like to swim laps. Circular and kidney-shaped pools are also popular. The bigger the pool, the more maintenance, heating and cleaning that are required. Sometimes all you really need is a small dipping pool to cool off. These types of pools are low maintenance and practical.

This pool has a shallow "beach entry" rather than steps.

Infinity-edge pools are extremely popular in Hawaii. They are especially dramatic on a view lot where the edge truly blends into the horizon. Pool owners should be aware that infinity-edge pools require more water due to excessive evaporation. They also cost more to build and to heat. Additionally, the trough that catches the water can turn into a stagnant eyesore of debris and bird droppings if it's designed poorly. Discuss with your pool contractor what type of trough will work best for you so this doesn't happen.

Vinyl pools are soft to the touch and therefore require a special vacuum head for cleaning. Fiberglass pools are quick to install and generally cost less than a plaster pool. If you opt for fiberglass, make sure you ask about what to do if you ever have to drain the pool.

Some pools are designed with a "beach entry" alternative to steps. This increasingly popular option is ideal for children, the disabled or seniors. Turtle sculptures, waterfalls and fountains can also be incorporated to create a fun and interesting environment.

Plants are located far enough away from this pool so that debris and leaves don't present a maintenance headache for the pool owner. Interlocking pavers are contrasted with cement coping for a sturdy, durable deck.

POOL DOS AND DON'TS

Falling leaves. Destructive tree roots. Leaky planters. Overlooking these possibilities and opting for aesthetics over practicality, some mainland architects will try to convince you of the merits of their landscaping ideas. But you are the one who has to live with the reality of a problematic pool resulting from impractical landscaping, poor design and other factors.

When it comes time to design your pool, avoid costly mistakes that you'll regret later.

Plants

One of the biggest mistakes you can make is to plant trees, hedges and lawns too close to the pool. Every time you trim your hedge, leaves will fly straight into the pool, sinking to the bottom and promoting algae. The wrong tree near your pool will shed foliage so badly that your pool will always be messy, the filter will become clogged and the chemical balance will be affected.

Large palm trees planted next to a pool can become a nuisance. Palm trees should be located at least 20 feet away from the pool because their roots will travel under the deck in search of the nearest water (your pool), undermining the concrete. Also, some varieties of palm trees shed heaps of annoying berries into the pool year round.

Grass next to the pool may look nice and feel good on the feet, but grass clippings will fly in the pool when you mow, and you could be tracking fertilizer into the pool from the soles of your feet, promoting black algae.

Equipment

Don't skimp on cost with a cheap pump, filter or motor. A quality system will give you years of trouble-free operation, as opposed to lesser equipment that will break down or lack sufficient horsepower to do the job. Make sure your system is installed in an area that is easily accessible, and that the PVC pipes do not block access to equipment.

To save on electricity, it is tempting to lessen the recommended amount of time your pump should operate each day. Unless you want your pool to turn green or get beslimed with yellow algae overnight, set your timer accordingly.

Pets

One of the most damaging and unsanitary things you can to do to your pool is let animals swim in it. Many pool service technicians will refuse to service a pool used by dogs. Dog hair wreaks havoc on the filter and parts of the pump, while the dog's oils, fur and skin can promote swaths of yellow and other-colored algae on the plaster surface of your pool.

MAINTAINING YOUR POOL

To maintain your pool's daily appearance, an automatic pool sweep is worth the expense. There are several models to choose from. Some of the newer high-tech models are quite efficient and less cumbersome than the old-style sweeps.

A pool sweep is not a substitute for weekly cleaning. In Hawaii during the rainy summer months, it's almost impossible to go for more than a week without pool maintenance before noticing yellow algae forming on the sides and bottom of the pool. From chemical treatments and testing to brushing and vacuuming, your pool professional will know exactly how to prevent and/or combat any situation that may come up.

Chlorine

Chlorine tablets are the standard for chlorinating your pool. You can float them in a floater or put them in the skimmer basket. After handling tabs, make sure you wash your hands thoroughly. If you rub your eyes, the powdery residue will sting for days.

More and more pool owners are discovering the benefits of salt makers to make chlorine. A salt-maker unit ranges from

$2,500 to $3,000 and, once installed, is relatively easy to maintain. With a salt maker, the odor and irritating effects of chlorine on the skin and eyes are diminished. It also keeps your pool cleaner more consistently, as long as you maintain the proper levels of salt and stabilizer/conditioner (cynuric acid). Fifty-pound bags of salt must be added every so often to maintain the right chlorine balance.

Algae Treatment

If yellow algae is visible on the sides and bottom of your pool, it needs to be brushed and treated with Yellowtrine or Shock. Yellow algae is a common problem in Hawaii.

Black algae forms conspicuous black specks that actually take root in the plaster. Scrubbing each spot with a wire brush will remove it, but treatment with black-algaecide will likely be necessary if you have a lot of spots forming quickly. This is a job for a pool professional, because some black-algae removers will actually strip the color from dark plaster surfaces, leaving white spots. Black algae can grow from dust, fertilizer, bird feces and other outside elements that land in the pool. If you have a pile of dirt near the pool, it is the likely culprit.

A pool that turns completely green demands the expertise of a professional who can rescue the water over several visits. Just because your pool has turned green doesn't automatically mean you have to get it drained, though. Get a second opinion if somebody tells you that draining is the only solution.

Lava-Rock Features

Lava-rock features and waterfalls add a beautiful Hawaiian touch to a pool, but they can be a maintenance headache if they are not properly designed or well placed. You want a lava-rock feature to be above water. Don't let yourself get talked into having one that is submerged under the water: it takes up space, sheds debris, holds bacteria, eats chemicals and will grow algae. Additionally, lava-rock features sometimes accumulate a white silica discoloration at the waterline that can't be removed.

The beauty of a waterfall cascading over lava rock cannot be denied, so accept the fact that there will be some permanent silica buildup if you choose to add a waterfall. Avoid turning your lava-rock feature into a planter. The dirt will simply leach into the pool and create a mess of algae and stains.

Create the perfect back-yard getaway by adding a water feature to your new or existing swimming pool and bring the sounds of nature to your own backyard.

Border tiles

Border tiles at the top of the pool will generally accumulate a white line of silica buildup at the waterline. It's one of the most difficult things to remove. You can use a pumice stone designed especially for cleaning pools and slowly grind it off by hand, but it is nearly impossible to keep it from coming back. This is because Hawaii water already contains a high amount of silica. A little silica buildup is inevitable, so consider having white tiles installed that will camouflage any potential discoloration.

KEEPING YOUR HEAD ABOVE WATER

Understanding the amount of maintenance and expense involved with pool ownership will help you decide what size and type of pool will work best for you. Make sure it's worth your while to own a pool by factoring in how much it will cost you per month versus how much you will actually be using it.

Most of all, if you have small children, make sure you've considered every safety precaution possible to prevent accidental drowning.

Spas

Swim spas produce a non-turbulent swim current that adjusts from a gentle flow to a racer's pace. It can be used for swimming, exercising and physical therapy.

Bubble, bubble, toil and trouble? Not so with today's portable spas—they're incredibly easy to install. You just wire them in and they're ready to go.

Portable spas (also called "self-contained") are by definition located above ground. However, you can achieve a built-in look by installing the spa partially into a surrounding deck, for example.

As the name suggests, in-ground spas are considered permanent and are usually part of an accompanying swimming pool. The filter, pump and heating system are located away from the spa, unlike the portable spa, which has everything built in. One benefit of the pool/spa combination is that if your pool is chlorinated with a salt maker, the spa will be too, resulting in less chlorine odor and less irritation to the eyes and skin. Best yet, if the spa has a waterfall spilling into the pool, the spa water will help heat the pool.

WHERE TO PUT YOUR SPA?

A typical three-person spa weighs about 2,500 pounds with water. If you're thinking about putting your spa on the lanai, check with a licensed contractor to make sure your lanai is shored up enough to support the weight of the unit. No matter the location, a solid, level foundation is essential.

The spa should also have access to a garden hose (that's what you'll use to refill it) and be located near a dedicated electrical outlet. Most portable spas run on 120 volts, but if you have any doubts about your circuit's capacity, check with a licensed electrician. The outlet you use for the spa must be part of a 20-amp circuit that doesn't service any other heavy-draw appliances.

Some spas have the option of running the equipment on 240 volts, which will increase the heating speed of the spa and allow the hydrojets to run for longer periods. To convert to 240 volts, a new circuit must be hard-wired to the spa by an electrician or spa contractor.

Make sure there are no trees or foliage close by that can drop debris or sap into the spa. A spa surrounded by dirt or grass will end up with dirt and grass tracked into it.

If you are thinking about placing your spa indoors, consider the potential pitfalls. Water will accumulate around the floor, making it slippery when wet. Proper drainage is required; hence a floor drain should be part of the plan. Good ventilation is essential because humidity from the spa may damage walls and promote mildew.

A pool-and-spa combination is an ideal situation because the hot water spilling over from the spa will help heat your pool water.

Interior spas should have plenty of ventilation, like these awning windows that offer lots of airflow. Good drainage is another important factor for an indoor spa.

WHAT KIND?

With portable spas, the quality varies by brand, so look for a product that is top of the line and carries a good warranty. Going the cheap route will likely bring you disappointment in the long run. Pick a spa that will suit your needs. If you want to entertain large groups, the deluxe family models with plenty of seating are the way to go. A deeper tub with few contours is good for exercising, while a tub with lots of massaging jets and comfortable seating is the choice for relaxation. There's also the swim spa, in which you can swim in place against a constant current.

Because of the heat and the amount of chemicals involved, in-ground spas often need to be resurfaced every six years or so. Depending on the brand, portable spas hold up well over the long haul but can be susceptible to cracking or discoloration from the sun and chlorine.

MAINTENANCE

A spa requires thorough weekly maintenance and a bit of shock treatment each week to keep it clean. The chemicals used are pretty much the same ones swimming pools need. You'll need to keep the pH balanced and test for alkalinity. Most of the newer spas also come with an ozonator that helps sanitize the water. For optimum performance, a spa should be drained and refilled every two to three months.

Tiki Torches

A Night Out: Amid the tropical ambiance provided by inline propane tiki torches, a down-to-earth landscape of ferns, palms, ti and banana plants complements the pool and deck of this Hawaii Kai home.

The tribe has spoken: there's nothing like the exotic ambiance of a tropical tiki torch on a hot Hawaiian night. Whether illuminating pathways, casting warm light at a poolside gathering or lighting the way to a luau, tiki torches are a shining symbol of the power and magic of Hawaii after dark.

Anyone can achieve this magic with a simple bamboo torch that costs as little as $6. These days, though, many Hawaii home-owners are installing more elaborate inline propane systems like those used at hotels and resorts throughout the Islands.

Tiki torches illuminate
the evening sky above
Kealakekua Bay, casting
a golden glow on a pool
deck that still glistens
from a late-afternoon
rain shower.

INLINE PROPANE TIKI-TORCH SYSTEMS

If you want to install an inline propane tiki-torch system in your yard or at your poolside, the first person to call is a licensed plumber. That's right, a plumber.

Because gas pipes are involved, a plumber needs to provide and install them, as well as determine the appropriate layout before putting them in. Depth requirements vary according to county or city plumbing codes. In Hawaii County, the minimum depth is at least 12 inches below the finished grade. Concrete is usually added around the base of each torch assembly to stabilize it, while the area around the base can be covered with gravel, sand or cinder.

The torch system is connected directly to the propane tank through its own line. Make sure the plumber pressure-tests the lines to detect any leaks.

In Hawaii, torch heads are sold statewide at local Airgas Gaspro outlets. The heads are made of copper with brass fittings and come in one standard cone shape. Airgas also carries assembly parts, including low-pressure regulators, rubber hoses and quick connects.

Although a shut-off valve is not a standard feature, you should add one to each torch. The valve, which is installed on the shaft, allows you isolate a single torch for illumination, repairs or mishaps without having to shut down the entire system. Everyone in your family should be instructed on how to turn off the torches in case of emergency.

How many torches you install is a matter of personal preference, but keep in mind it doesn't take many torches to illuminate a yard at night. If you have too many torches, you might find yourself feeling like you're standing in the middle of a very well-lit birthday cake!

Once a torch system has been operating for a while, the homeowner should occasionally inspect the orifice inside each cone to make certain there aren't insects or spiders blocking it. It's normal for soot to accumulate on the heads because the torches are made to burn that way, but to prevent soot buildup, you can try brushing the heads every once in a while.

According to The Gas Company, one torch head rated at 18,000 BTUH (British thermal units per hour) will use approximately five gallons of propane per 20 hours of burn. The torch heads should be kept four feet away from foliage and branches and away from umbrellas, canopies and the like. As captivating as the dancing orange flames of the tiki torch are, always remember that you're dealing with fire, so take the appropriate precautions.

PORTABLE PROPANE TORCHES

Instead of an expensive inline system, you can opt for freestanding portable propane torches. Fueled by a five-gallon propane cylinder that can be concealed with a covering, the portable torch sits on a base made of quarter-inch steel and comes in single-, double- and triple-headed designs. Portable stands range from $140 to $280 and are manufactured by Kona Industries, which specializes in this type of torch.

These torches are great for the beach, luaus, gatherings, and for your yard and pool area. They're frequently used by hotels and resorts for special events because they are portable.

BAMBOO TORCHES

Mainstays in Hawaii, the humble, inexpensive bamboo torches sold at hardware stores are good to have around. They are basically bamboo poles with citronella-oil canisters on top. The flames help keep bugs away while creating the same romantic ambiance as high-end torches.

The end of the bamboo pole is cut at an angle so it can be driven into the ground. Be careful, because the pole can easily be knocked down, and if left in the dirt for too long, it can rot at the base. Found online, patented torch stands shaped like pyramids can be filled with sand to add weight.

To affix poles to your lanai railing, you can make your own tiki-torch holders out of six-inch PVC pipes. Drill two holes through both sides of the pipe, then screw the pipe into the railing at a 35-degree angle. Make sure the torches are positioned away from awnings, eaves and umbrellas. Use only an extended lighter to light the torches, not a BIC lighter or matches. ❖

Simple bamboo torches feature citronella canisters to keep mosquitoes away while creating the same tropical ambiance as an expensive propane torch. To affix poles to your lanai railing, you can make your own tiki-torch holders out of PVC pipes.

Beat the Heat

Air Conditioning

Y ou can minimize the need for air conditioning by installing ceiling and wall insulation, by utilizing natural ventilation and ceiling fans, and by having a cool roof over your head. But the fact remains, many areas of Hawaii are simply too hot to live in without air conditioning, especially during the spring and summer months when humidity is high and the Hawaiian sun is at its most intense.

Air conditioning can actually improve indoor air quality because it pulls air from the outside and filters it. This can be helpful for people with respiratory ailments and allergies and those who are affected by vog and smog. Your AC can also function as a dehumidifier, helping to keep your house dry and free of mold.

KEEP IT RUNNING RIGHT

Many people don't think about their air conditioning until it doesn't work—like when the in-laws are visiting and there's suddenly no AC in the guest bedroom.

Air-conditioning units require maintenance to keep them running properly. The salt air, humidity, mold and corrosion factors in Hawaii will definitely impact your system. Semi-annual or quarterly maintenance by an AC professional is recommended. If you are a snowbird homeowner, your AC unit still needs to be maintained on a regular basis, even if it's sitting dormant for half the year.

Proper maintenance includes checking the outside condensing unit and gauges, replacing filters, cleaning the grills, removing dust from the coils and checking the pressure. The pressure should not change. If it's lower, it means you have a leak. If it's high, it could indicate that the compressor is on its last legs. If you are purchasing a new house, be sure to get the maintenance records on your AC from the previous owner.

Keeping mold out of the unit is a big concern. One of the best options is to add a UV light to the existing fan coils to keep the mold and mildew down. Instead of throwaway filters, opt for higher-quality pleated or electrostatic filters. For do-it-yourself maintenance, change the filter every 30 days if you live in a high-pollen or high-dust area.

Newer residential air conditioners are a lot more energy efficient than old models. Some central AC systems manufactured in 2007 have more than twice the energy efficiency of older systems.

THE ABCS OF AC

It takes more than one tradesperson to install an air conditioning unit, as an AC contractor is generally not licensed to do the electrical, only the installation and hookup. If your house needs to be re-wired for AC, you'll probably need different contractors to complete the project. An upgrade to your electrical service may also be required, which could involve the electric company's transformer and service wiring at additional costs.

DUCTLESS SPLIT SYSTEM

If you're retrofitting an existing house for air conditioning, the best application is a ductless split unit. After a house is built, it would be really expensive and in some cases near impossible to install air ducts for central AC; therefore, ductless is the preferred option.

The split type of system includes one or more remote-controlled decorative wall-mount units inside the house and a remote condensing unit outside. The main advantages of split systems are their small size and flexibility for zoning or cooling individual rooms when needed. Many models can have as many as four indoor air-handling units connected to one outdoor unit, each capable of operating in individual rooms only when needed.

There are many options with the split system. A one-zone system in the master bedroom is an affordable way to start. You can add to it at a later date when you want to cool more rooms. If you need air conditioning in larger spaces like a kitchen, dining room and living room combination, you'll need the larger ductless split system.

Air conditioning is measured by BTUs. There are 12,000 BTUs in a ton of air conditioning. Split systems come in locked sizes—the typical size for a medium-sized home would be a 30,000 to 36,000 BTU system (or three tons). If you want to start out with a 12,000-BTU system, there is a dual-zone option where you can have one outside condensing unit for two small bedrooms and an inside remote-controlled decorative wall-mount unit for each bedroom.

In Hawaii, Sanyo and Fujitsu systems are popular brands. Mitsubishi manufactures the top-of-the-line zone ductless system, considered the "Rolls Royce" of air conditioners. New variable refrigerant flow multi-splits from Daiken allow you to have several inside air handlers and one outside condensing unit.

CENTRAL AIR CONDITIONING

For central AC to be effective in Hawaii, the home should be insulated enough to be able to contain the conditioned air. If you're planning for AC, make sure ceiling, wall and/or floor insulation is installed during construction, or you can install a radiant barrier of insulation under the roof to help keep the ducts cool.

Central air conditioning is a ducted system that can usually only be installed when the house is being built. It circulates cool air through a system of supply and return ducts: the supply ducts carry the cooled air from the air conditioner to

the home and, as it circulates through the house, the warmer air flows back to the air conditioner through the return ducts.

Carrier Corporation is on the cutting edge of energy-efficient systems, which feature humidity controls and two- and three-speed inside-air-handling units. UV lighting, which kills mold and mildew at the backside of the fan coil where it is moist and dark, can be added to most all air conditioning systems. Some Carrier models feature comfort zones with automatic dampers that open and close when rooms are not occupied, and in fact, comfort zone systems can be added to any of the Carrier residential split systems to increase efficiency. The company is also the first to use environmentally sound Puron® refrigerant in a full line of air conditioning for improved energy efficiency.

Central air conditioners are more efficient than room air conditioners—plus, they are quiet and easy to operate. If you have an older central air conditioner, you might choose to replace the outside compressor with a high-efficiency unit, or replace the entire system to match the indoor unit, especially if it's a new-model residential split system. If your air conditioner is only 10 years old, you could save 20 to 40 percent in energy costs by replacing it with a newer model.

Central air conditioners are rated by their "seasonal energy efficiency ratio," or SEER. Older systems have a SEER rating of 8.5 or less. In accordance to new energy standards, residential air conditioners manufactured after January 2006 must have a SEER rating of 13 or higher. Carrier Corporation is now making units with SEER ratings up to 21.

If you have an older central air conditioning unit, you might try replacing the outside compressor with a high-efficiency unit. Doing so could save you up to 40 percent in energy costs.

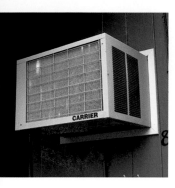

Window units are effective for cooling individual rooms, especially during the hot summer months. For best results, make sure the unit is placed in a shaded location.

ROOM OR WINDOW UNITS

Window units are designed to cool a specific room for a short period of time and are most often used during the hot summer months. Do your research before you purchase one. If it's not ranked in the top five in Consumer Report, don't bother.

To operate efficiently, a window air conditioner should be placed in a shaded location, such as on the north side of the home. An air conditioner exposed to direct sunlight will use five percent more energy than one that is in the shade. Make sure there is a tight seal between the window and the unit. Filters should be cleaned periodically and coils kept clean and free of debris. Use a vacuum cleaner to suck up dirt, dust and leaves from around the coils.

PORTABLES

The cheapest way to air-condition a room is with a portable unit, but in actuality, they don't really work that well and can suck up electricity. Additionally, you'll need to attach the unit to a large hose to discharge the heat from the house. Stay clear of units with unrecognizable names, which could be made with paper-thin Freon piping. If it ruptures or the compressor fails, you'll have to replace the entire unit. Panasonic makes a good portable that is rated high on the consumer lists.

TYPES OF AIR CONDITIONERS

• DUCTLESS SPLIT SYSTEM— COOLS ONE OR MORE ROOMS, WITH THE COMPRESSOR OUTSIDE AND THE FAN COIL UNITS INDOORS. UNITS ARE USUALLY MOUNTED ON THE CEILING, FLOOR OR WALL.

• CENTRAL—AN AIR-DISTRIBUTION SYSTEM THAT LOWERS THE TEMPERATURE OF THE ENTIRE HOUSE BY CARRYING COOL AIR TO ALL ROOMS.

• PORTABLE—DOES NOT REQUIRE INSTALLATION AND CAN BE MOVED FROM ONE ROOM TO ANOTHER. HOT AIR NEEDS TO BE VENTED OUTDOORS.

• ROOM OR WINDOW—COOLS A SINGLE ROOM WITH THE UNIT MOUNTED THROUGH THE WALL OR IN A WINDOW.

Ceiling Fans

A ceiling fan uses the same amount of electricity as a 100-watt light bulb and will make a room feel cooler by at least eight degrees. The blade pitch should complement the size of the motor—the bigger the motor, the bigger the pitch.

In Hawaii, not only does a ceiling fan bring a tropical ambiance to the home, it can cool a room significantly and can help to prevent mold by keeping the air circulating throughout your house.

AIRING ON THE SIDE OF CEILING FANS

The good news is, a ceiling fan generally uses less electricity than a 100-watt light bulb and can make a specific area feel cooler by an average of eight degrees. Ceiling fan/light combination units that have earned the Energy Star rating are about 50 per-

Tropical fans with
Hawaiian motifs such
as these pineapple light
fixtures are the ultimate
in Hawaii-style living.
When cleaning blades,
avoid using anything
moist that could warp
the blade.

cent more efficient than conventional fan/light units.

A good fan should last at least 15 years. Cheap fans from box retailers or hardware stores generally don't last long in the tropics. Cheap fans also have low angles to their blades, thus moving less air, and it's also harder to find replacement parts for them.

If you live in a wet elevation, you'll definitely want to get a fan that is wet-rated or damp-rated, manufactured either with resin, plastic, or powder-coated steel motor housings. Resin or plastic housings combined with plastic blades hold up best in Hawaii because they will resist rust and moisture absorption.

The best measurement of a fan's performance is the CFM, or cubic feet of air per minute. The better-performing fans on the market start at 7,000 CFMs.

The next thing to look for is blade pitch, followed by blade size. The blade pitch should complement the motor size—the bigger the motor, the bigger the pitch. For a room larger than 12 feet by 12 feet, go with a blade size of 52 inches or more. For smaller rooms, 44-inch blades are sufficient. Today's manufacturers are now making fans with blades as big as 72 inches. These are best placed in extra-large rooms with high ceilings.

If you want to go for the exotic look à la Casablanca, most of the tropical-style fans with wicker blades are better for decorative purposes than performance, since they don't move as much air.

Most ceiling fans have a reverse switch that allows you to draw the air up or down. In Hawaii, fans are best left the counter-clockwise position, which blows the air down.

INSTALLATION AND MAINTENANCE

The distance the fan should hang from the ceiling depends on the height of the ceiling. Placement is often dictated by personal preference, but generally the top of the fan housing should be anywhere between nine to 10 feet off the floor. Stems or "down rods" are manufactured up to six feet in length. A four-foot down rod will accommodate a 14-foot ceiling, a three-foot down rod a 13-foot ceiling and so on. Most fans have at least 78 inches of wire to play with, so if you want something longer than six feet for that ultra-high ceiling, you can connect two down rods to make an extension.

It might be challenging to find an electrician locally who will deal with ceiling fans, but if you are a confident do-it-yourselfer, it's not hard to install one yourself. Once your fan is operating, be sure to clean the blades regularly. With wood blades, you'll want to dry-dust them rather than using water because the blades could end up warping.

Keeping a fan balanced can sometimes be an issue. If you notice a wobble, it usually means a screw is loose or the blade arm is bent. Sometimes tightening a single screw can fix the worst fan wobble. In the case of a bent blade arm, though, you'll probably have to replace it.

Reducing Heat in the Home

Hear that hissing noise? It's the sound of your hard-earned money flying out the window, thanks to the high cost of air conditioning.

Sure, it gets hot in Hawaii. But there are plenty of things you can do to dramatically reduce the heat and damaging UV rays that enter your home.

KEEPING YOUR ROOF COOL

Good planning starts at the top, which means your roof. A normal roof keeps the sun out, but a cool roof keeps heat out too, reducing or even eliminating the need for air conditioning.

If your house is like many in Hawaii, it's got a metal roof. Today's metal roofing technology has come a long way, and features such attributes as Ultra-Cool reflective coatings that can reduce heat penetration into the attic by 36 percent. This is good news if you prefer a darker-colored roof, which traditionally attracts more sunlight. White, of course, is the coolest metal roof possible.

Of all the roofing materials out there, asphalt shingles tend to attract the most heat to the house. Ironwood shingles are touted to offer some of the best insulation against heat among roofing products.

Under Hawaii's searing sun, a roof can reach 150 degrees, which will then transfer to the ceiling and toast the house and its occupants. Good insulation is essential for a cool roof and can lower ceiling temperature by 18 degrees, making a room feel at least nine degrees cooler. Types of insulation include:

- Fiberglass
- Foam board
- Radiant barrier block

Each of these products helps keep heat from gathering on the roof and entering the attic and/or ceiling.

If you opt for fiberglass insulation, you should go for the six-inch thickness (R-value 19). It's best used for new homes, as it is costly to install into existing framed ceilings.

Foam-board insulation works well for open-beam ceilings where other types of insulation cannot be used. It should be installed at least two inches thick and be either R-10 or R-14 rated.

Resembling a big piece of foil, a radiant barrier is stapled to the roof framing, either inside or outside the frame, with the shiny side down. This is the least expensive of the insulation options. A radiant barrier with an emissivity rate of 0.05 is recommended for Hawaii.

ATTIC VENTS

Attic ventilators are small fans that remove hot air from the attic. For homes with attics, ventilation is essential, especially if you have a radiant barrier installed. Fans located on the peak of

By removing hot air from the attic or a cathedral ceiling, a solar-powered attic fan like this Cyclone model can lower the interior temperature of the house up to 20 degrees. You can also earn a 35-percent state energy tax credit on the cost of the fan.

the roof provide the best results. There are several different types of vents:

• Ridge vents help pull hot air out of the attic.
• Eave vents allow fresh air into the attic.
• Gable vents pull air through the house from both directions.
• Solar-powered attic fans can earn you a 35-percent state energy tax credit. These fans work hardest when the sun is its strongest.

KEEPING YOUR WINDOWS COOL

All that sun and UV streaming through a Hawaii window will most certainly damage or fade wood floors, rugs, artwork, photographs and furniture. Window tinting helps solve the problem.

Tinted Window Film

Just about any type of window can be tinted with film. Depending on the shade of the film, you can achieve a 78-percent reduction in heat coming through the window. Window film can also block 99 percent of damaging UV rays.

Tinting reduces glare (daytime TV watchers take note) as well as bright sunlight, helping to keep things comfortable all day long. You'll be able to maintain that great view and not have to close the blinds or shades. Film also has the added benefit of creating a kind of safety glass and might even provide some sound-proofing.

When choosing the brand of film to be installed, examine the products closely. The differences in quality will be apparent. 3M, the company that invented window film in the 1960s, excels at manufacturing top-quality plastic and glue and provides a lifetime warranty against bubbling, peeling, cracking or chipping. The 3M "Night Vision 25" is a popular choice in Hawaii.

Tinted Glass

With tinted glass, the color is actually part of the glass. Tints come in gray, bronze and various other shades. Green/blue tints are the most cooling. Tinted laminated glass has a PVB layer that reduces heat penetration and also keeps out almost 100 percent of damaging UV rays.

Double-paned or insulated windows are tricky in Hawaii. When your home is sealed up during the day, insulated glass can actually make the home hotter by trapping the heat. The moisture

in the air can also fog the glass between the panes. Be sure to get the "tropical" or "low-e squared" type so this doesn't happen.

Shutters and Blinds

Window coverings not only offer unlimited decorative possibilities for your home's interior, they keep harmful UV rays from entering the home and help to lower interior room temperatures. Shutters made of Polywood are actually manufactured with insulating materials in the product. Unlike traditional wood or synthetic shutters, Polywood is made with a baked-on finish that's easy to clean.

Natural Ventilation with Windows

The right window combined with Hawaii's cool trade winds will keep your home comfortable all year round. With proper placement and window style, you can actually direct trade winds through your home. Casement, awning and jalousie windows all provide excellent ventilation. When positioned appropriately, a casement window can act like a "wing" outside the house, catching the breeze and bringing it right into your home.

Retractable awnings
provide shade when you
need it, like at this home
in Keauhou-Kona. In
addition to keeping your
patio or lanai shaded,
it's like adding a room
to your home.

MORE COOL SOLUTIONS

The side of your house that faces direct sunlight will heat up...and fast!

Creating shade with awnings, eaves, roof overhangs and landscaping is the logical solution. Trees, trees, trees! Trees that cast shade across your house are the best source of cooling possible. Shading the south- and west-facing windows of your home goes a long way toward reducing heat in the kamaaina home.

Eaves and roof overhangs are other important components of a cooler house. Because the sun is lower in the sky to the south, windows and walls that face south should have a roof overhang that casts a 45-degree shadow when the sun is at its peak, which will provide the most shade cast across the wall and windows. Use a 70-degree angle for overhangs above windows that face north.

Awnings come in all different colors, sizes and styles. Some retractable awning systems can provide up to 480 square feet of shade when you need it, creating coolness and protection over windows, doors, decks and lanais while protecting outdoor furniture from fading and deterioration. Plus it's like adding a room to your home.

Wall insulation is essential if you have air conditioning. A rating of R-11 is recommended for wall insulation in Hawaii. There's also the option of a radiant barrier, which is simply stapled on the inside or outside of the framing.

Screens

Available in motorized or manual-powered styles, sophisticated executive retractable screens come in sizes as large as 16- by 25-feet. The screens are ideal for large windows with beautiful, unobstructed views.

Hawaii residents generally rely on open windows to cool their homes and keep the ventilation flowing. No doubt about it, window screens are a staple of life in the Islands. Technically, the window screen is called an "insect screen," for obvious reasons. Not only does a screen keep the bugs out; it lets the fresh air in.

Even though they are susceptible to corrosion, aluminum frames are the norm for screened windows and doors. The screen industry has yet to come up with a viable alternative that is as light and flexible as aluminum, yet strong enough to serve as a frame for screens. The two strongest types of aluminum frames are anodized and powder-coated.

If maintained properly and washed regularly, aluminum screens can last for 30 years in Hawaii. If not maintained, they can deteriorate in just a few years.

To maintain a screen, all you need to do is take it down and hose it off every six months. This will remove any salt build-up that has settled at the bottom on the frame and begun corroding it. At the same time, you're removing the dust that accumulates on the screen cloth, which can attract mold and block ventilation.

To further protect the frame from corrosion, you can try applying a penetrating oil to the surface.

ANOTHER FINE MESH...

Screens can be made to fit any size of window. Your screen professional will take the measurements, go back to the shop and create a perfectly sized screen that fits tight and snug into the window. For a really bug-proof fit, have your screen installed with a "lip" frame.

Screens keep out most bugs, including ants. But when gnats come around, those little buggers can fly through the finest standard weave. Tighter-mesh screens are available but offer less ventilation. Some island residents have a second set of screens on hand with tighter mesh and switch out during gnat season.

There are different types of screen cloth available, but fiberglass is the most common. Vinyl-coated polyester is a relatively new product and is highly durable. The ultimate screen for durability is the "pet screen," designed to withstand all that scraping, clawing and pawing when your pet wants to be let in, not to mention that one aggressive Hawaii rat that might chew its way through a screen to get to your fruit bowl.

SLIDING SCREEN DOORS OF THE 21ST CENTURY

There has been some evolution in the sliding screen door designs, including stainless-steel rollers that last longer than conventional rollers. The aluminum frame, however, is still the dominant product utilized because it is strong and lightweight. There

State-of-the-art retractable screens allow complete ventilation and the ability to disappear from view when they're not being used.

are many new aluminum designs that are both attractive and durable.

Keeping your screen door open all night can be a security risk, but if you want that extra ventilation, consider investing in a popular but expensive new product: the security sliding screen door made of heavy-duty security mesh.

Because it's not possible to completely eliminate the small gap between the sliding screen door and the glass door, though, you will never truly be able leave a screen door open all night without the chance of a bug crawling in. Even with the tightest fit possible, there still has to be a gap of 1/4 of an inch between the screen-door frame and the main frame in order for the door to move.

Pocket sliding screened windows and doors slide out of sight into the wall. In Hawaii, you have to make sure that pocket is kept free of debris, insect nests or gecko eggs. And it's not easy to get your vacuum attachment into that pocket!

DISAPPEARING ACT—RETRACTABLE SCREENS

Similar to the old-style rollup shade, the retractable screen is a spring-loaded contraption whereby the screen, when tugged,

The horizontal retract-
able screen snaps into
place from side to side,
and is a good choice
for doorways where a
swinging screen door
would be awkward.

rolls into a housing tube that is mounted either vertically or horizontally. When drawn, the screen is usually latched magnetically.

The retractable screen works best for specific applications.
For windows or lanais, a "pull down" or vertical screen that
retracts from top to bottom is most appropriate. The horizontal
retractable screen, on the other hand, operates from side to side.
This is a good choice for double-French doors and other types of
doorways where a swinging screen door could be awkward.

A great place to install a horizontal retractable screen is at a
doorway leading from the garage into the kitchen. When it's time
to unload those bags of groceries, you don't have to deal with an
annoying swinging screen door.

A horizontal retractable screen door, however, does not do
well in windy areas, as there is no track at the threshold to hold

it in place. Additionally, bugs can crawl through the bottom. The vertical retractable screen, by contrast, will latch at the floor.

When shopping for retractable screens, do your research. These products need to be of the highest quality in order to hold up for the long haul. Ideally, the screen should be lightening-quick when it snaps back into the housing. As for repairs, the mesh can easily be replaced, as can the springs. To ensure the life of the product, keep your retractable screen lubricated with silicon spray. Retractable screens need to be kept clean of bugs, dog hair and dust as well.

For the high-end home, a motorized retractable screen exudes a certain James Bond appeal. Simply press the button on the remote control and watch the screen disappear into the beam. The vertical tracks can also be concealed inside a column, beam or post. If you're nervous about how a motorized product will hold up in Hawaii, there is always the choice of a manual crank, but manufacturers say that that motorized components are well protected inside the beam.

Either way, you can go as large as 25 by 16 feet with these executive-style screens, which are especially suited for spaces between house and patio to foster a Hawaiiana-style, open-air ambiance.

SECURITY SCREEN DOORS

Security screen doors made of steel may look like Fort Knox, but they don't last long in Hawaii and are rust buckets waiting to happen. When investing in a security screen door, go for the heavy-gauge extruded aluminum frame. It won't rust and is better suited to the tropical elements. The sculptured grille should withstand bending, breaking, smashing and pulling—as well as those pets wanting to come in. ❖

Battling
the Elements

Bug-Proofing for the Tropics

There's no getting around it—bugs are a fact of life in Hawaii. Whether you own a million-dollar home or rent a humble coffee shack, you don't have to face a losing battle trying to prevent pests from entering your home.

Vigilance and preparation are the keys to success. The first line of defense is to shore up all entry points where bugs can find their way in. The secret weapon: caulk.

SEAL THE DEAL

A four-pack of acrylic caulk can go a long way toward preventing infestations. Take time to caulk every last crevice and gap in beams, ceilings, baseboards and walls to keep spiders, centipedes, roaches, pill bugs, millipedes and other uninvited guests out. Even if you need four-dozen tubes of caulk to get the job done, it will be worth the effort.

Be sure that your screens are free of rips or holes and that they fit tightly into the window. Screen-repair kits include patches that you can place over holes and sew onto the screen. If that doesn't do the job, you'll want to replace the entire screen altogether. Try installing screen mesh over unused floor and sink drains as well as around rooftop vent pipes and other awkward entry points in the laundry room, kitchen or bathroom.

Bugs often enter your house the same way you do—through the door. Make sure there is as little space as possible beneath your exterior doors by installing an insulating strip at the bottom to eliminate the gap. Sliding screen doors should be inspected to ensure there's a tight fit. Bugs can get in under the tracks of a closed sliding glass door. If this is happening, apply 100-percent silicone sealant to any suspicious areas for a waterproof seal. If you have a metal security door, the tighter-mesh screens work best to keep gnats and mosquitoes out.

Of course all the prevention methods in the world won't help if you leave food or garbage out for extended periods of time. If you don't have a garbage disposal, try bagging your food scraps in the freezer until garbage day or your next trip to the transfer station. Keep surfaces clean and wiped down, and store opened packages of food in airtight plastic containers or sealed jars. Vacuum-sealed vaults designed for dog food work great in the kitchen for storing rice, grains, sugars, teas and cereal.

The best way to keep bugs out of the house is to ensure that all gaps and openings are sealed and screens are free of rips and tears. Window screens installed with a lip frame provide better protection against intruders like ants.

Your bug-battling kit should include boric acid, the local's choice for combating cockroaches (opposite) in the home.

ASSEMBLE YOUR OWN BUG-BATTLING KIT

In the tradition of the standard first aid kit, every home in Hawaii should be sufficiently supplied with the necessary bug-battling tools to handle any situation. A good bug kit might include the following: boric acid, Raid, wasp spray, rat traps, mosquito coils, fly swatter, roach baits, Sevin powder, a rubber mallet and a machete. If you're averse to using poisons, alternative substances like diatomaceous earth, orange citrus oil and vinegar can be effective for pest control.

Boric acid is the people's choice for getting rid of cockroaches. Sprinkle the powder in every corner, along the baseboards, in drawers and behind the refrigerator. Within two weeks, cockroaches will be gone. Boric acid kills by removing moisture from the body of the target pest, causing severe dehydration. Sprinkle it where it won't get scattered around and keep it away from dishes and food.

A second line of defense is to place poison roach baits under sinks and in corners. If you find dead cockroaches on their backs, you'll know you're doing something right. Some pets are sensitive to the vapors emanating from Combat™ roach traps, so if you're using them, watch for possible nausea or lethargy in your pet.

For ants, a 50/50 mixture of boric acid and sugar can be left in a few small piles overnight. Ants will take the mixture back to their nests and poison their colony.

ALTERNATIVE SUBSTANCES

An EPA-approved powder, diatomaceous earth (DE) kills crawling insects around the house and near your pet. Made of fossilized shells, it acts like ground glass, slicing through the joints of the insect. Although extermination is not instantaneous, it will help slow down infestations of fleas and ticks. You can sprinkle it around the outer perimeter of your house. Take care when handling DE because it's known to cause lung cancer. You might have heard that you can dust your pets with DE for fleas, but this isn't actually a good idea.

Some Hawaii residents have discovered the power of citrus oil to control ants, roaches and fleas. GreenSense Citrus Oil is made of naturally occurring ingredients derived from orange peels. It can be sprayed on floors, carpets, interior sur-faces and outside. The citrus fragrance repels pests, and the oil's waxy substance causes suffocation to the insect while burning its exoskeleton.

Mint oil works to slow pests down. Additionally, a mixture of water and vinegar sprayed around an area will temporarily repel ants.

Though you might not believe it, a machete and a rubber mallet are essential tools to have at the ready. The rubber mallet is perfect for smashing a centipede without damaging your floor. The flat edge of the machete is useful for scooping up millipedes and flicking them out the door—as well as for scraping up the remains of a smashed centipede.

Bugs Bugging You?

CENTIPEDES

There's nothing more alarming than the sight of a fast-moving centipede scurrying across the floor. That's when all of your internal alarm bells sound off and you begin frantically searching for the nearest heavy object to smash it to smithereens.

The aforementioned rubber mallet is the weapon of choice for killing a centipede. Slicing the centipede in half with a machete or steak knife will only result in the disturbing sight of two halves running in opposite directions or, worse, multiple chopped-up segments still wiggling hours after the kill (not to mention a deep gash in your floor). A mallet, on the other hand, can be aimed directly at the head...if you can figure out which end is the head!

Smashing only the head instead of the entire body will result in a clean kill and less of a mess to scrape off the floor. Don't be deceived by the tail, which coils upward when the centipede is threatened. It is a decoy to divert attention from the head, where the "biting" legs or pinchers are located. Centipedes are nocturnal meat eaters, hunting at night for bugs and using their pinchers to paralyze their prey. Through evolution, the centipede's first two legs have become specialized pinchers with ducts for venom. The venom contains a histamine with protein toxins that can cause cardiac arrest in laboratory animals.

When a centipede stings you, it leaves two puncture marks in the skin. Centipedes are not life threatening to humans, but the sting can cause pain that lasts for six to eight hours or more. Swelling and bruising can occur. A tube of prescription Topicort (Desoximetasone 0.0% Gel Tar) is good to have on hand for treating the sting. The quicker it's applied, the less severe the reaction may be. Seek medical attention if you have an adverse reaction to any bug bite.

There are a number of different species of centipedes in Hawaii—24, to be exact. The centipede is actually not an insect, but a distant relative of the crawfish. Local lore suggests that the sting of the tiny purplish-blue centipede packs the biggest punch, but the enormous "garden centipede" is a frightening sight for even the most seasoned Hawaii resident. These reddish-brown creatures can grow up to nine inches long and live more than five years.

If you live in a centipede-prone house, make sure you pick up wet towels and washcloths off the floor, as centipedes are attracted to dark, moist hiding places. Shake out your shoes and

Centipedes have one pair of legs per body segment but only an odd number of body segments, never even. Therefore a centipede can never live up to its name of "centi" (100) and "pede" (feet) because there's no such thing as a centipede with 50 body segments.

your gardening gloves, too. Centipedes have been known to hitchhike into the house after a trip to a warehouse store where boxes stored on cement floors offer safe havens for the shy creatures. They also like to hide in bunches of bananas.

To control centipedes, make sure the openings to your house are sealed tight. Keep lumber, rubbish and piles of rocks a safe distance from your house. Rock gardens, potted plants and cardboard boxes near the house also attract centipedes, as do compost and mulch. The inside of your house can be made hostile territory for the centipede, where it will find little food and water but plenty of weapons like a barbell, hammer or rubber "slippah" ready to be smashed upon it. Centipedes are seeking cockroaches and other insects to eat, so keeping your house bug free will help keep centipedes out.

If you have a bad problem with centipedes, consider stocking your yard with a few chickens. This is an effective permaculture solution because chickens enjoy feasting on them.

Many pest-control professionals have acquired a secret appreciation for centipedes and speak highly of their ability to combat cockroaches and other bugs. The centipede, with its varied patterns and intriguing anatomy, is a creature of interest. If you feel at all benevolent toward the much-maligned centipede, rescue it from your house with a pair of hot-dog tongs and place it outside in the garden where it belongs. Because it feeds on roaches and slugs, consider it a beneficial creature for your yard.

An "odd" fact about centipedes: the word "centipede" literally means "one hundred feet," but you'll never find a centipede with exactly 100 legs. That's because centipedes have only an odd number of body segments, never even, with one pair of legs per segment. So despite its name, the centipede can never have 100 legs because it can never have 50 body segments.

MILLIPEDES

Ask any pest-control professional which bug is their least favorite, and they will likely tell you that the lowly millipede is the worst of the lot. Chickens in your yard won't help eliminate them because millipedes are so disgusting, even chickens, ducks and other birds won't eat them. In short, they are very hard to control.

About two inches in length, the reddish-brown, worm-like millipede has two pairs of legs per body segment. When threatened, it will harden and curl up like a watchspring. Feeding on

Millipedes have a short lifespan but are difficult to combat during the height of millipede season. Attracted to light, they are especially prolific at night, so keep your porch light off if you are trying to keep them from entering your home.

rotting organic material, millipedes are seeking heat when they enter your house. If they get into your house at night, they will crawl to the nearest source of heat and light, including right into bed with you, and attempt to curl up under your arm. This is not the kind of bedroom action anyone wants!

Millipedes secrete a noxious substance that can stain your floor and will also burn your skin or, worse, leave a curly millipede "tattoo" or scar that resembles a case of ringworm. The disturbing truth is that they will crawl to the warmest part of your body: up your shorts, into the crease of your neck or even into your mouth or ears while you are sleeping. Because you can barely feel one when it is crawling on you, chances are you won't know it was there until you wake up with a burning sensation and a curly mark on your skin that can take weeks to fade.

Millipedes infest certain areas of Hawaii, while other areas don't get them at all. Late fall/early winter is the prime season for millipedes, and, as with plagues of locusts, there are occasional years when millipedes are more prolific than other years.

Vector Control will tell you to keep your yard free of rotting organic material if you want to control millipedes. But the fact is, if you live in a millipede zone, they will come crawling toward your house en masse and even up the side of your house to the second story to enter any way possible, whether your yard is trim and clean or not. Be sure to keep your porch light off at night if you are battling millipedes during high season.

Sevin bait sprinkled in the yard may do some good, but Sevin *powder* is the locals' preferred method for killing millipedes. If they are continually getting into your house through your sliding glass doors or other entry points, sprinkle a two-inch-wide barrier of Sevin powder around the perimeter of your foundations. Each morning, you'll need to sweep away the curled carcasses of dead millipedes. If, despite this precaution, you find one in your house, scoop it up with a flat edge and toss it in the toilet or outside. Don't pick them up with your bare fingertips; they will burn your skin.

Cane spiders may look frightening but they are actually harmless, gentle creatures. Be careful dealing with a cane spider that has a sack of eggs underneath it, however. You just might unleash dozens of baby spiders that will scatter hither and yon.

CANE SPIDERS

While they are menacing in appearance, cane spiders are benign, shy, fragile creatures, even though they can sometimes grow so big they resemble a human hand! Like ocean crabs, they move fast. The best way to remove a cane spider from your home is the "bowl and cardboard" method. Place a large Tupperware bowl over the spider, slide a thin piece of cardboard underneath and gently take the spider outside. Their legs are easily broken, so handle them with care. More distressing than the sight of a giant cane spider is the sight of a giant "amputee" spider with missing legs. In Hawaii, it's considered bad luck to kill a cane spider.

CARPENTER ANTS

These aggressive pests are some of the toughest insects to combat in Hawaii. Unlike those in other parts of the U.S., Hawaii carpenter ants do not consume wood, but they will establish nests in hollowed-out rotting wood and other hidden spots. They feed on small insects and food found in the home, including meat and grease. They've also been known to ransack paper products like stationery supplies and old paperwork.

Often confused with the termite, the carpenter ant can be identified by its telltale narrow waistline and crooked antennae. Spraying rogue ants won't solve the problem. Find an entry hole in the wall or door and spray Term-Out (with the flexible hose and needle nozzle) into the hole, and put out ant bait. In serious cases, rotten woodwork and paneling must be replaced. If you see stray wings around the house, you know that the carpenter ant population has grown in size and is looking for new places to nest.

PAPER WASPS AND YELLOW JACKETS

Prevalent at sea level, paper wasps are attracted to water and build nests in the eaves of your house. Use the can of wasp insecticide specially designed to spray the nests from a distance like a laser. It works! The best time to spray wasp nests is at night when they have all returned to the nest. Wasps are not active at night and will be less likely to fly at you. If you see wasps loitering around your pool, fencing, railings, sheds or other areas, first zap the nests, then make sure that you plug up or caulk any gaps in structures where wasps will return. Eliminate all mud nests hanging from the eaves and elsewhere. Wasps will return to unoccupied nests time and again.

If you have ground wasps (yellow jackets), don't attempt to treat them yourself. Call Vector Control. They will come to your house and treat them with a restricted-use pesticide.

Wasps like to build mud nests in the eaves of homes. Spray active nests at once, then knock the nests down so wasps don't return. Left: Honey-bee swarms should be dealt with by a local beekeeper. Call Vector Control for a list of beekeepers in your area.

HONEY BEE SWARMS

Common in Hawaii, honey-bee swarms can be a menacing and scary thing to have in your yard. At the height of the season, which runs from spring through summer, hives get larger and bees begin to swarm, looking for a new place to start a hive. Call a beekeeper to come out and collect the bees. Vector Control has a list of beekeepers in your area. If you ignore the problem and the bees establish themselves in your attic, wall or crawl space, you will need to have them exterminated by a pest-control company.

CARPENTER BEES

What's that huge round hole drilled into your valuable ohia post or the side of your house? It's the nesting orifice of the carpenter bee, a large flying insect that resembles a bumblebee. Like the name suggests, these busy creatures are veritable power drills when it comes to damaging your wood. Exposed, unpainted wood is an easy target, particularly redwood. You might even find a deep hole averaging 3/8 of an inch in diameter, about the size of a dime, drilled straight into the handle of your broomstick or fruit-picking pole.

Because they have no stingers, male bees are not a stinging threat but do tend to buzz around people. A male be can be identified by its yellow face. To combat the nuisance males, spray them directly with wasp spray. Female bees stand guard at the entry of the holes. The females have stingers, but more importantly, they are the ones that bore the nests that threaten your structure. They will also crawl between the cracks of siding and roofing and inflict untold damage behind the scenes.

A bee hole typically measures an inch or two in depth, and might then turn 90 degrees where the egg chamber is located. Eggs are laid at the end of the chamber, which is sealed tight by the mother bee. Some egg chambers can be two or more feet in length, with additional tunneling and chambers branching off from there.

You can trap carpenter bees in a jar attached to a block of wood. They will crawl through the decoy hole and die in the jar. Keep a dead bee in the jar at all times to attract additional bees to the trap.

Carpenter bees return again and again to old nests; therefore, it is imperative that you treat the holes. For active nests, use an insecticidal dust such as Drione Dust, which adheres to the hairs on the body. Unlike liquid insecticide, dust will also remain intact outside the sealed chamber awaiting emerging larvae. Problem holes with long chambers might require a special applicator that can force the dust deep into the nest.

Holes can be sealed with a mixture of epoxy and sawdust, then sanded and refinished. Unfortunately, sealing one hole might drive the bee to make a new one. Some Hawaii homeowners have found success with traps made from a jar and a block of wood that matches the wood of their house. To make a trap, take the lid of a small jar and screw it to one side of the block. Drill a bee-hole-sized hole through the lid halfway into the block, then drill another hole into the other side of the block to meet it. Bees will crawl through the hole and die in the jar. Keep a dead bee in the trap to lure other bees.

Because carpenter bees are attracted to exposed wood, make sure all wood surfaces are painted. Old-timers in Hawaii applied diesel to the exterior of their redwood catchment tanks to deter carpenter bees permanently.

MOSQUITOES

Mosquitoes are a year-round problem in Hawaii. There are lots of mosquito-control products on the market, so check around for the most appropriate one.

Coils are commonly used outdoors as repellents and are most effective when lit in advance of "mosquito hour." Two new skin repellents for mosquitoes, picaridin and lemon eucalyptus oil, have recently been approved for use in Hawaii by the U.S. Centers for Disease Control and Prevention. They, along with the familiar DEET, are now available in certain repellents. Off! and Cutler now make lemon-eucalyptus-oil products. Picaridin, which is odorless and not oily, was introduced in the U.S. in 2005 for the first time. Avon's Skin-So-Soft is also still widely hailed as an effective skin repellent.

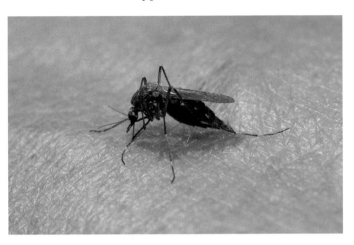

If itch and irritation aren't reasons enough to avoid mosquitoes, disease and infection should be. Although West Nile virus has yet to reach Hawaii as of 2007, there was an outbreak of dengue fever, also carried by mosquitoes, in 2001-2002. Additionally, scratching bites can lead to possible infection.

Standing water is the best-known culprit for attracting mosquitoes, whether it's in a pond, rain barrels, buckets of water, pet water dishes, swimming pools, the bottom of planters and any place where water accumulates. Mosquitoes also like moist, shady areas under the lanai, in garages and in dense foliage. With a little effort, you can locate precisely where pockets of mosquitoes exist around your house.

There are myriad mosquito products designed specifically for treating different types of areas. The options are endless, from larvicides, repellents and sprays to foggers, powders, incense, granules and heavy-duty aerosol machines. But remember, if you are battling severe infestations, you must first address the reproduction sites where larval stages are taking place rather than simply relying on repellents or zappers.

If you have mosquitoes inside your house, indoor mosquito

Mosquitoes need to be dealt with at the source. Look for breeding sites in moist, dark places under the lanai, or in standing water like puddles, ponds and rain barrels.

traps are effective. Certain traps involve the use of standing water and dissolvable tablets that replicate a scent attractive to mosquitoes. You might notice that mosquitoes can gather in closets. The scent of the human body on clothes can lure them to hover inside.

SCORPIONS

Scorpions are usually found at sea level in Hawaii. They hunt at night and hide out in dark, dry places during the day. A prime location for scorpions is inside those old cardboard boxes folded and stacked in your garage. The key to preventing infestation is to keep clutter to a minimum.

The sting of the scorpion is not threatening but can be painful. The scorpion has 10 legs—the first pair is its pinchers. The tail is an extension of the abdomen and is where the stinger is located. The scorpion grabs its prey with its "lobster claw" pinchers and then curls its tail over its body and injects the venom. Fortunately, scorpions in Hawaii are less dangerous then their counterparts in Arizona, and their sting is usually no worse than a bee sting.

The gold-dust day gecko may look cute, but in large numbers they can be real pests in the kitchen and throughout the home.

GOLD-DUST DAY GECKOS: FRIEND OR FOE?

The beautiful green geckos with the colorful markings sure are pretty, but for some residents of Hawaii they have become real pests, infesting homes in large numbers. Not unlike mice, they root around in the kitchen and get into food, sweets and trash, leaving gobs of drippy gecko poop on the walls. What's more, they are rapidly decimating the population of "good" geckos known as "house geckos" or mo'o, those famous chirping geckos that arrived in Hawaii with the first Polynesians and are considered a good luck sign in the home.

Conversely, a few of these green critters in your house might not present that much of problem. They do eat bugs. And many people balk at the idea of killing the beautiful and cute green creatures, which have been elevated to pop-culture status by the Geico commercials.

Because they are active during the day, gold-dust day geckos capture food and nesting space from the nocturnal house gecko. They also attack and eat them—like many reptiles, they are cannibalistic, feeding on their own kind. Additionally, the green geckos carry liver flukes that can infect cats that eat them.

An invasive species from Madagascar, the gold-dust day gecko was reportedly intentionally introduced in 1974 in Honolulu by a misguided reptile specialist who thought it make a great addition to the Islands. Now found statewide except for Lanai, the green gold-dust day gecko first appeared in the Punchbowl area and spread from there. In the last few years, the population has exploded in Kona. The invasive species committee on Maui is working to target a few populated areas like Kihei and Lahaina, where one home recently had an infestation of more than 300 inside and thousands more in the yard. On Molokai, the control efforts appear to be keeping them at bay.

Of primary concern to state officials is the fact that dense populations of green geckos, as well as of coqui frogs, would provide an unlimited food source for the dreaded brown tree snake should it ever get loose in Hawaii, virtually guaranteeing its proliferation. The gold-dust day gecko is considered a restricted animal in Hawaii. It is illegal to transport it.

There's also the giant Madagascar day gecko now found in some areas of the state. It can be distinguished from the gold-dust day gecko by the red polka dots on its back and the red cross-bands on its head. It can reach 14 inches in length and will bite. The gold-dust day gecko, by contrast, has the same green coloring but has three red teardrop markings on its hips, blue around the eyes and a sprinkling of yellow specks.

Pest-control companies report that fumigation is not effective for treating infestations of gold-dust day geckos. That's because the gecko can manipulate its breathing process to survive the gas. Some residents recommend using sticky traps baited with a sugary cereal like Froot Loops.

determine the exact location of the call. The good news is that the frog will puff up when threatened, making it a little easier to capture than when it's flat. Additionally, the frog tends to stay in one place rather than roaming around the yard.

After you capture a frog, drop it in a baggie and put it in the freezer for 24 to 48 hours to kill it. Although frog hunting is a time-consuming activity, it's the first thing you should do to keep the frogs out of your yard before resorting to Plan B: pesticides.

Pesticides

The only legal pesticides to combat the coqui frog are citric acid and hydrated lime. For residential purposes, hydrated lime must be sprayed in three-percent liquid solution. Don't use it in areas where children play. Also avoid spraying it where ammonium-containing fertilizers have been used, because the lime can react with fertilizer and release ammonia gas.

Additionally, hydrated lime shouldn't be applied to trees that may drip the chemical on people, automobiles and property. Most importantly, don't apply it to food crops.

People using the spray are required to wear protective clothing, gloves, eyewear and respirators. On the Big Island, sprayers are available on loan from the county. Maui has sprayers available through the Department of Agriculture.

Warning: hydrated lime is poisonous to the human respiratory system. Some residents are violating the guidelines by applying the dust form of the chemical in their yards. Not only is this illegal, it can be deadly!

Citric acid is available at garden stores and chemical distribution centers. It is mixed in a 16-percent solution with water and is much more user-friendly than hydrated lime, but it's a lot more expensive.

Form a Frog Squad

If you suspect coquis in your neighborhood, don't delay. Come together as a community, form a frog squad and act quickly so you can stop them. Quick and vigilant action is the key to preventing the spread of this highly invasive pest.

Corrosion

Corrosion happens quickly in Hawaii and can be a safety hazard if left unchecked. Corroded bicycle wheels, rusty ceiling fans and rotting light fixtures are all the situations that can spell danger if ignored for too long.

Whether it's attacking something as small as a screw on your lanai or as large as the foundation of your house, corrosion is a destructive force that can be more than just an eyesore; it can lead to safety hazards for you and your family.

With salt air and high humidity, rust is a fact of life in Hawaii. A broken bolt on swimming pool slide, a rusty ceiling fan, a rotting light fixture, a cracked pipe, a pitted rain gutter or a leaky metal roof—any of these situations can spell danger if corrosion is ignored for too long.

OUTDOOR CORROSION

House Exterior

Debris like leaves and dirt can lead to corrosion, so it's important to keep your home's exterior clean and dry. Keep plants and trees away from the roof or the exterior and make sure rain gutters are clear. Use only a high-grade paint for your exterior, and keep it well maintained.

Exposed metal surfaces should be protected with paint. For a rusty metal surface, sand it with an electric grinder, then brush on a layer of Osphlo, a conversion coating available at marine stores. Let it dry, apply the primer to the metal and then paint.

Pipes

Brittle, corroded pipes can result in costly water damage to your home. Pipes will corrode when two different metals are joined together, such as a copper water pipe connected to a steel water main. The same is true for brass and copper fixtures connected to steel pipes, or a steel screw installed in a brass faucet or an aluminum rain gutter. When installing plumbing, make sure that the pipes and joints are made of the same material. If that's not possible, place a plastic or fiber connector between the joints to keep the metals from touching.

Spalling

Spalling occurs in concrete when rusted reinforcement iron and brackets expand and then break the concrete apart. Contractors are now using galvanized rebar or rust-resistant metal embeds to prevent the problem. Metal should be at least three inches deep into the concrete, and the concrete should also be sealed.

Outdoor Furniture, Tools and Equipment

Garden tools, lawn mowers, nuts, bolts, bicycles, lanai furniture and light fixtures are all susceptible to instant corrosion in Hawaii.

Keeping your equipment and furniture clean and free of dirt and other contaminants is the first line of defense. You can also try painting over metal surfaces or coating them with lacquer. Painting over any nicks or pits that occur will protect exposed metal.

Exposed metal surfaces should be covered with paint to prevent corrosion. There are marine-grade coatings available that can be applied before adding primer and paint.

Penetrating oils can also be rubbed onto metal or aluminum surfaces like sliding screen doors, hinges and the like.

To clean up rusted tools, use steel wool dipped in penetrating oil. You can also coat tools with motor oil, or make your own protective coating with equal parts of petroleum jelly and lanolin heated in the microwave and mixed well. Apply while still warm.

CORROSION ON THE WATERFRONT

Sun. Sand. Surf. There's nothing like the joy of living on the oceanfront. And nothing like the maintenance headache for oceanfront homeowners when corrosion takes hold and never lets go.

Although dealing with rust is often a losing battle when living on the water, homeowners can take measures to prevent and control corrosion.

Windows and Doors

Vinyl windows and vinyl sliding doors hold up over the long haul against the brutal effects of sea spray and salt air. The windowpanes themselves are glass, but the frames and tracks are manufactured of specially formulated vinyl that requires no maintenance or painting.

Honolulu-based Coastal Windows manufactures a brand of vinyl windows and doors specifically designed for the island climate. Their sliding windows ride on a Teflon strip instead of wheels, and their sliding doors and sliding screen doors also hold up against corrosion. If you live on the oceanfront, vinyl is the only practical solution for windows and doors; otherwise, you'll just be replacing your sliders year in and year out. Remember, aluminum will pit, wood will swell, but vinyl is final!

Appliances

Instead of spending $500 on that top-of-the-line ceiling fan for the inside of your oceanfront home, buy the exterior fans specifically made for patios. They will last three times longer.

Stainless steel will rust on the oceanfront, so even top-quality appliances are not immune to corrosion. If you live right on the water in an open-air setting, settle for the cheap toaster, coffee grinder, TV, stereo and other electronic equipment because they will soon need to be replaced—guaranteed. Unless you have a specially insulated room, you don't want thousands of dollars'

worth of expensive computer equipment or electronics on the
waterfront.

For larger kitchen and laundry appliances, you might try
applying a clear coat of urethane on exposed surfaces. Cast-iron
sinks are a good investment. For sliding closet doors, silicon
spray on the tracks will keep things well lubed. Products like
Corrosion Block can prevent corrosion from forming.

Telephone wiring is especially vulnerable by the water. Be
sure to maintain an insurance plan with the telephone company,
because interior wire repair is only a matter of time.

Exterior

Salt air will eat the varnish off your house's trim, turning it
black. Use paint instead of stain or varnish, which are a waste
of money and labor on the oceanfront. Paint over nails, brackets
and screws.

A roof made of tile or composite asphalt will last longer by
the beach than a metal roof. It's also important to keep the exterior of the house well painted, caulked and sealed.

Bronze light fixtures and sconces will hold up better than fixtures made of other metals.

Mold

Mold that grows under eaves should be pressure-washed away so that it doesn't end up creeping into the interior of your home. A little elbow grease will also take care of the problem.

In Hawaii, mold can take hold at any elevation. Whether you live in a multi-million-dollar estate at sea level or a ramshackle rental upcountry, it doesn't take much to attract mold.

Every year, mold is headline news in Hawaii. In 2003, Hilton Hawaiian Village spent $55 million to eradicate mold in the 453-room Kalia Tower in Waikiki. In 2002, by a bizarre coincidence, mold invaded both the Honolulu and Washington, D.C., offices of U.S. Senator Dan Inouye, forcing the senator to occupy temporary quarters for more than a year.

In 2004, a massive infestation overtook the University of Hawaii-Manoa's Kennedy Theater, caking the entire theater in a thick, slimy, green layer.

For homeowners, a bad incursion of mold (also called mildew) can lead to severe allergies and respiratory ailments, unpleasant odors and costly structural repairs. With the high humidity and plentiful rainfall in Hawaii, it pays to know how to "break the mold."

PREVENTING MOLD

Damp, dark places are susceptible to mold. Keep your exterior free of debris and make sure water is diverted at least three feet away from the house.

Outside the Home

The elements necessary for mold to grow include humidity, lack of airflow, excessive moisture, decay, darkness and a food source such as paper, fabric, leather, drywall, wood, lint—just about anything that collects dust and holds moisture.

Maintaining good air circulation outside the house is important. Don't plant trees too close to the house. Not only will they block air circulation, they can promote decay on your roof by dropping seeds, pods, leaves and stems, which can lead to a leaky roof and rotting wood.

Because mold can work its way into the house from the outside, exterior maintenance is essential. Paint your house with a high-end exterior paint that has mildewcide in it. Make sure all exposed or rusty surfaces are primed and protected as well. If you live in a wet elevation, add mildewcide to the paint even if it already contains it.

Always use a base coat to prime new surfaces. Cheap paint and stain will break down quickly, leading to mold. Never paint over existing mold! It will only continue to grow.

Black streaks on the roof could be an indicator of mold. Red mold on the outside of your house is the most difficult to kill. If you have any type of mold on your exterior, though, pressure washing is the best way to remove it. Because this is a hazardous job, it's best to hire a professional, who will use plain water or a fungicide mixture to hose down the exterior siding and eaves. You can also attempt to clean it off with water, detergent and elbow grease, or with trisodium phosphate (TSP) mixed with bleach.

If mold becomes established in the wood, dry rot may form. When the mold dies, the wood dries and then shrinks, breaking up into irregular chunks and creating a nightmare for homeowners. Cracks in the wood fiber create a siphon for moisture, carrying it to the undamaged portions of the wood. Left unchecked, this process can cause severe structural damage requiring complete removal and replacement of walls and other structures.

Fix all leaks immediately. Improper drainage of water toward a home can lead to water intrusion in foundations, crawl spaces and concrete slabs. Gutters and downspouts should be clear of all debris, and water should be diverted at least three feet away from the house.

Inside the Home

Closing up your house for long periods of time can promote mold. Homes belonging to snowbirds in Hawaii are especially susceptible if homeowners cover their furniture and close up their houses for an extended period of time. They return from the mainland only to find that mold has gone crazy on curtains, furniture, cupboards, counters, floors and walls.

Moisture, darkness and lack of air circulation are the three prime factors for promoting mold. One of the best ways to prevent its spread is to make sure that air is continually circulating through the house. Ceiling fans, attic vents, bathroom exhaust fans and screened windows all do the job. Keeping your house clean and dusted is also important, as mold will grow on dusty screens and furniture. If you live on the ground floor, wall-to-wall carpeting is probably not a good idea in Hawaii.

Closets are a prime location for mold. Many Hawaii homeowners actually remove the closet doors so that air can circulate and sunlight can shine in. Sunlight is one of your best weapons against mold. Wire mesh shelves are also helpful in keeping air flowing. Clothes should not be packed too tightly inside a closet, a situation that leads to mold faster than anything else. One piece of mildewed clothing will infect the entire closet.

If your clothes become moldy, you can try hanging them in the sun before washing them. Leather belts, shoes and purses are also prone to mold. Wipe them down and set them in the sun. If you have a leather jacket that is moldy, you might want to take it to the dry cleaners. Don't keep moldy items festering in your drawers or closets.

When upholstered furniture becomes moldy, sometimes the only option is to toss it. The same holds true for pillows, mattresses, carpeting and curtains. Just get rid of them. You might try brushing them off and putting them out in the sun, but more than likely, you won't eliminate the problem.

De-humidifiers and gel paks are helpful in capturing moisture. A dehumidifier can be plumbed so that water automatically empties outside and away from the house.

BATTLING MOLD

Okay, so you have mold. Now what? Don't panic. Yes, there are some highly toxic forms of mold out there—like *Stachybotrys* or "toxic black mold," a fungus that emits chemical poisons that become airborne and cause serious health problems and even death.

Chances are, though, that the mold you're dealing with isn't life threatening. You can deal with the small-to-medium areas yourself. Remember, mold is a spore that will fly through the air. Therefore, you should scrub and wipe the area directly rather than using a spray bottle that might scatter the spores.

Misconceptions about Bleach

Bleach is not an EPA-registered fungicide and is not recommended for cleaning mold directly. The variable conditions of the water, surface, contact time and organic material must all be right for bleach to work as a disinfectant. Bleach alone may temporarily help, but it begins to deactivate as soon as it comes in contact with the mold. Bleach in combination with laundry detergent is a better option.

SOLD ON MOLD

Fear of mold is growing as fast as mold itself. That's why mold can be "gold" for certain manufacturers of air purifiers touted to combat it, or uncertified mold inspectors who ratchet up the fear factor about mold in the home.

If the moldy area is small and well defined, you can do the cleanup yourself as long as you don't have health problems or allergies. If mold is extensive or is growing behind walls or under floors, contact a professional.

The safe and complete removal of a serious mold problem requires the service of a professional. After removal of mold-damaged materials and the use of fungicide, an antimicrobial coating is used to prevent future mold growth. It's costly, so do what you can to prevent mold before it takes over for good.

MOLD-REMOVAL TIPS

Clothing and Fabric

HANG THE FABRICS IN THE SUN AND AIR THEM THOROUGHLY. TREAT WASHABLE FABRICS WITH LIQUID LAUNDRY DETERGENT AND HOT WATER. USE CHLORINE BEACH IF IT'S SAFE FOR THE FABRIC.

IF YOU HAVE SPOTS OF MOLD ON UPHOLSTERED ARTICLES, TRY SPONGING THE SURFACE WITH SOAPY DETERGENT AND WIPING IT CLEAN. OR USE A CLOTH MOISTENED WITH A 50/50 MIXTURE OF DILUTED ALCOHOL AND WATER.

Walls

FOR PAINTED WALLS, SCRUB WITH A SOAPY SOLUTION OF DETERGENT AND BLEACH IN WARM WATER. DRY THOROUGHLY. FOR WOODWORK, DRY THE WOOD WITH A HAIRDRYER, WIPE OFF THE MILDEW AND SCRUB WITH A DETERGENT SOLUTION, OR A CLEANER. DRY THOROUGHLY.

Shower Stall

MIX POWDERED LAUNDRY DETERGENT WITH A QUART OF BLEACH AND THREE QUARTS OF WARM WATER. SCRUB WITH A HARD BRUSH, RINSE THE AREA AND THEN DRY IT THOROUGHLY.

Shower Curtain

PUT IT IN THE WASHING MACHINE ON A GENTLE CYCLE AND ADD ONE CUP OF BLEACH. TO COUNTERACT THE BLEACH, ADD ONE CUP OF VINEGAR TO THE RINSE WATER.

Rats

Some rats are so aggressive they will actually chew through a screen to get inside. A thick wire mesh will keep them out of problem places.

Oh, rats, another sleepless night in Hawaii!
There's nothing more disconcerting than knowing you have a rat in the house. How it got in is one story; how to get rid of it is another story entirely. Depending on the size of the rat, you can use a sticky trap, a snap trap, or something more sophisticated to catch it.

GETTING RID OF RATS

Sticky Traps

The problem with sticky traps is the animal is still alive and struggling when caught, which means you'll have to sink the whole trap-rat combination in a bucket of water to drown the rat and put it out of its misery.

Sticky traps tend to catch other critters as well. Be sure to re-seal your opened box of sticky traps, or you'll have a mess of dead cockroaches and geckos to deal with next time you open the box.

Snap Traps

The bigger the rat, the less likely the sticky trap will work, as larger rodents just tend to drag them around. That's where the snap trap comes in. Although bloody and violent, the snap trap is made in extra-large sizes licensed to kill. Place the trap under a piece of cardboard along the baseboard, away from pets and children. Rats move at night, feeling with their whiskers as they travel along the wall. So be sure to place the trap perpendicular to the wall.

Peanut butter or nuts are often used as bait, but sometimes the rat can snag them and escape unharmed. Shredded meat or chicken will stay in place longer, forcing the animal to sit and gnaw the bait before the strong arm of the law comes smashing down.

Cleanup is gruesome, no doubt about it. Double-bag the sucker and take it to the nearest transfer station for disposal. Be sure to wear gloves when handling the remains. Wash and clean the used trap thoroughly—rats will avoid a trap that has the scent of a previous kill on it. If a used trap continually fails to draw the next rat, you might have to toss it and start fresh.

Electronic Traps, Ultrasonic Devices and More

Blood and guts inside the house is not the ideal situation. But as the old saying goes, there's always someone trying to build a better mousetrap.

The electronic rattrap is a less hands-on method for catching a rat. Some brands operate on batteries and have a red indicator light when the batteries are low and need to be replaced. The trap activates when the rat touches the metal plates inside the one-way housing, where it becomes trapped and hopefully zapped.

Ultrasonic rat chasers emit high-frequency sound waves touted to repel rodents. The sound is inaudible to people and pets. Most of these devices plug directly into an outlet.

Cats in the yard are an excellent low-tech method of eliminating rats. Unfortunately, they like to show off their catch by leaving it at your doorstep in a bloody pile, a job well done. Finally, if you would prefer to catch a rat to set it free rather than kill it, there are live "Hav-a-Hart" traps on the market big enough for the job.

Poison Bait

Using bait to catch rats poses a dilemma. You have to consider the possibility of secondary poisoning should a dog, cat or bird eat the bait or the poisoned dead rat. Your local garden shop should sell a bait box that is animal proof except to rats. Make sure the station doesn't get wet, or the bait will get moldy.

If you decide to use rat bait, put it outside only. If you use it inside your house, you will likely end up with a dead carcass rotting somewhere behind your refrigerator out of reach.

PREVENTING RATS

In Hawaii, certain roofs are prime nesting destinations for rats. If your roof is particularly open, it could be a rat motel waiting to happen. With some metal roofs, you need to make sure you have rubber closures blocking all entry tunnels.

Obviously, doors and windows must have a nice, tight fit. There should be no wide gaps around the plumbing. However, some rats are so aggressive, they will actually chew through your screen to get to that fruit bowl sitting on your counter. If this is happening, you'll likely have to replace the screen with thick wire mesh.

Rats can also chew through plastic garbage cans. A metal can with a tight-fitting lid is a better option. Don't leave those big bags of dog food outside, either. Rats will chew right through them, as well as through boxes of old clothes left in the shed or garage. Imagine the feeling of opening that box of hand-me-downs only to find a filthy rat's nest inside.

If you are battling rats, you'll probably have no choice but to feed any pets inside—outdoor pet bowls are a beacon for rats. If that old sofa on your lanai has been soiled by rats, you can try cleaning and deodorizing it, but the sad fact is, rats will return to the scene of the crime again and again. When vacuuming rat droppings, be sure to wear gloves and a particle mask. Empty your vacuum cleaner immediately.

Rats can also burrow under slab-on-grade foundations. Dog kennels are particularly susceptible to intruding rats. Look for cracks and trails where they may be getting in.

Veritable roadways for rodents, tree branches touching the roof of your house always need to be trimmed back. (Rats will actually swing up and down on a branch and catapult themselves to their next destination.) Be sure to move lumber piles, firewood and other potential rodent habitats away from the walls of your home, as well as things leaning against the wall that rats can climb.

With all the fruit trees in Hawaii, rats have plenty to feast on. Clean up rotting fruit on the ground daily. If you see a rat's nest up in a tree and are not averse to using bait, place the bait somewhere near the tree. Put bird feeders with seed away from the house.

Snap traps are a violent, albeit effective way to kill a large rat. Often-times rats will detect the smell of a used trap and avoid it, so clean well after use or try a new one.

SIGNS OF RATS

- RUB MARKS ON WALLS
- GNAW MARKS ON STRUCTURES AND OBJECTS
- FECAL DROPPINGS
- A RUNWAY—A STEADY PATH OR TRAIL
- ODORS
- SLEEPLESS NIGHTS

Termites

Subterranean termite damage differs from that of drywood galleries in that the tunneling markings run along the grain of the wood as opposed to blistering and pocketing.

Inviting friends to dine at your home is one thing; inviting termites to dine ON your home is another thing entirely.

Statewide, termites inflict more than $100 million in damage each year. But many Hawaii homebuyers don't even think about getting their homes inspected until they have to—when their house is in escrow.

You can check for termites yourself, but a licensed pest-control professional will know exactly what to look for and where.

A reliable inspection should last several hours for a standard home and 45 minutes for a condominium. A good inspection will include all areas of your structure, including crawl spaces and attics. An inspector can also tell you if you're attracting termites to your home with rotting wood, leaky plumbing and other forms of neglect.

WHO ARE THEY?

When it comes to termites, it's important to know what species you're dealing with. Each has its own distinguishing characteristics, potential for damage and ways to be exterminated.

Of the seven known species in Hawaii, there are two main types to consider: drywood and Formosan subterranean (ground) termites.

By far the most destructive pest you will ever encounter in Hawaii is the mighty Formosan subterranean termite. An established colony of subterraneans is able to demolish an entire home in less than two years or eat the equivalent of one foot of a two-by-four in just a week!

Drywood termites, on the other hand, tend to go for the trim and other non-structural wood.

How to Tell if You Have Drywood Termites

Identified by dry, grainy droppings that vary color and are the consistency of sand, drywood termites can usually be found in the trim wood. Droppings are ejected out of the wood from the so-called "kick-out" holes inside the galleries and then accumulate in a pile below or are sprinkled across a windowsill or floor.

Just looking at droppings, it's easy to mistake ant activity for that of drywood termites. If you find brown piles that are fluffy and clustered, those are likely the result of ants.

Drywood termites assemble in relatively small numbers per colony—10 to 15 termites on average, up to 100 at the most. It's not always obvious how many drywood colonies might be residing in your house, or even if a colony is active. Damaged wood by itself may not be sufficient proof that termites are currently at work.

How to Tell if You Have Subterranean Termites

Unlike drywood termites, the subterranean termite does not leave droppings. These termites are so stealthy you may not even know you have them until you notice springy floors, hollow-sounding beams, warped walls, moist wood or blistered paint.

Subterranean termite galleries have tunneling markings that run along the grain of the wood, as opposed to drywood galleries that tend to blister the wood, leaving a pocket behind the paint. Drywood termites prefer the sapwood that's often used in trim and moulding, as well as the soft woods such as pine.

Drywood termites can be identified by dry, grainy droppings usually found on window sills, floors and trim.

The telltale sign of subterranean termites is the characteristic "mud tubes" made of fecal matter and mud running along the outside of your foundation, on boards, over masonry, on plumbing or even into trees, wood piles and fencing. Wood that comes in contact with the soil or ground is highly conducive to ground termite infestation.

If you find a mud tunnel on or near your house, do NOT attempt to treat the problem yourself by injecting store-bought termiticide into the tunnel. You will end up driving the worker termites to another area where they may gather in greater numbers and inflict more damage.

Swarms of termites in and around your house are another sign of infestation. In Hawaii, the swarming season for drywood and subterranean termites lasts from late March to mid-September. The subterraneans swarm in high numbers on warm, windless, humid nights between 7:30 and 8:30, attracted to light. They, like the drywood termites, leave their annoying transparent wings behind. Only two percent of the swarmers survive, but others travel in twos, burrowing into the ground to start a new colony.

If you see two termites traveling in tandem, kill them—they are attempting to mate.

THE DISTURBING TRUTH ABOUT SUBTERRANEAN TERMITES

It's a fact: subterranean termites can destroy an entire house in less than two years. While drywood termites might take at least two years to work their way through a foot of wood, subterranean termites can demolish the same plank in less than two weeks. You can replace an entire wall only to replace it again months later if subterranean termites are at work.

Drywood termites often feed on the non-structural wood like

the trim, door and window frames, doors, cabinets and shelving. Subterranean termites can and will attack the structural lumber and can actually impact the integrity of the building.

Subterranean colonies are located underground, sometimes up to 400 feet away from your structure. They house vast numbers, averaging between two million and, in severe cases, 10 million termites.

Arriving on Oahu in the late 1800s during the trading days, subterranean termites spread out to the other islands within a few decades, finally arriving in Molokai in 1975. They have an appetite for everything cellulose, including wood, paper, fruits, nuts and live plants. They will gnaw their way into anything to make their way to a food source, including electrical wires, plaster, plastic and linoleum. They'll even burrow through tiny fissures in concrete.

Even chemically treated wood is not guaranteed to be 100-percent safe from subterranean termites. Formosans are so aggressive that certain kamikaze members of the colony will sacrifice their lives to get to the untreated middle section of the wood so that others may feast.

TREATMENT OPTIONS

Fumigation and Tenting

Tenting kills 95 to 100 percent of drywood termites living in a structure, but it won't help much with subterranean termites— it only eliminates about five percent of the colony. That's because unlike drywood termites, the majority of the subterranean colony spends little time in your house. The few "workers" that are there will voraciously munch on foundation posts, beams and other structures and then quickly return to the colony with food to feed the rest of their clan.

With tenting, a gas called Vikane is released inside the home, penetrating the deepest part of the wood. Some pest-control companies charge a flat rate per cubic foot, while others base their rates on the conditions present in or underneath the structure that will determine the amount of gas needed. Houses located on porous lava rock, for example, might require more gas during fumigation.

After tenting, ants and geckos tend to gather to feast on the dead. Ask your pest-control company about additional services for dealing with the influx.

Termite companies across the Islands provide many options for exterminating drywood termites, including alternatives to fumigation such as localized chemical treatments with orange oil, foam termiticide or injected repellant and non-repellant termiticides. Spot treatment is useful for attacking small colonies of drywood termites. If you only have a few isolated small colonies, you may be able achieve control with localized methods and not need to go to the expense of tenting.

Treating Subterranean Termites

Liquid termiticide application, either repellent or non-repellent, is one control method. Termidor is a non-repellant liquid termiticide that is applied in a several different ways, such as trenching, drilling or injecting under concrete or other construction barriers. Depending on the home, the pest-control company may drill into the foundation slab and/or create a barrier around the house by trenching and treating around the perimeter. With non-repellent products, the infected termites will infect the rest of the colony through physical contact, grooming and feeding.

Baiting is the most requested as well as the most expensive method for treating subterranean termites. Bait stations such as Sentricon™, Exterra™ or Firstline™ are placed in the soil around the perimeter of your house and checked regularly for termite activity. Foraging members of the colony take the bait back to the colony and infect the others. Active ingredients range from a molting inhibitor that prevents growth to a slow-acting stomach poison that is undetected and freely shared.

Baiting programs require monthly inspections until the colony has fed successfully and collapses, usually within nine months to two years. There should be regular monitoring after the colony is destroyed, along with annual inspections.

Non-chemical methods include Basaltic termite barriers (BTB) that are made of a thick layer of basalt sand laid down before the slab is poured, through which termites cannot penetrate. A stainless steel screen, Termi-Mesh, blocks termites under the house and is applied over joints and cracks and around pipes. The woven mesh is too fine for termites to penetrate and too hard for them to chew through.

IMPASSE® Termite Blocker is a new product available through authorized pest-control operators. It is similar to BTB

Bait stations are placed strategically in the yard to combat subterranean termites. Regular inspections are needed until the colony has been eliminated.

and Termi-Mesh in that it must be installed before you build. The sleeves are secured around the plumbing and electrical penetration pipes and block the subterranean termites' access. The product is used in conjunction with the pre-construction termite soil treatment required by the building code, meaning that soil beneath slabs of new homes must be chemically pre-treated for termites.

Homeowners can disrupt the effectiveness of the soil treatment, however, by planting, raking or grating the perimeter surrounding the house. Ask the pest-control worker when it's safe to start these activities. ❖

PREVENTING TERMITES

THE NUMBER-ONE FACTOR THAT DRAWS SUBTERRANEAN TERMITES IS WATER. THERE ARE SIMPLE THINGS YOU CAN DO TO PREVENT TERMITES FROM GATHERING NEAR YOUR HOME.

• KEEP SHRUBS AND TREES CLEAR FROM THE HOUSE.
• MAKE SURE RAINWATER IS DIVERTED AT LEAST THREE FEET AWAY FROM YOUR FOUNDATIONS, TO OR BEYOND THE DRIP-LINE.
• KEEP GUTTERS AND DOWNSPOUTS CLEAR OF DEBRIS.
• AIM SPRINKLERS AWAY FROM THE HOUSE.

• FIX ALL LEAKY PLUMBING AND ROOFING.
• DON'T GATHER OR BURY SCRAP WOOD UNDER OR NEAR THE HOME.
• KEEP MULCH AWAY FROM YOUR HOME.
• MAINTAIN EXTERIOR PAINT.
• REPAIR GAPS IN EXTERIOR AND RIPS IN SCREENS.
• KEEP POTTED PLANTS A DISTANCE FROM THE HOUSE.
• DON'T BRING SOIL FROM UNKNOWN SOURCES TO YOUR YARD.
• BEFORE INSTALLING NEW CABINETRY, MAKE SURE THE WOOD WAS FUMIGATED.

Energy Efficiency

Energy-Saving Tips

HOW TO LOWER YOUR ELECTRIC BILL

The cost of electricity in Hawaii is higher than on the mainland for many reasons. Factors include higher fuel costs, the need for reserve-generating capacity, and the relatively small customer bases on certain islands, to name a few.

Rates vary from island to island. In 2004, Molokai and Kauai averaged the highest rate per kilowatt-hour at 25.74 and 25.6 cents per kWh respectively, followed by Lanai (25.15 cents), Big Island (23.91 cents), Maui (20.85 cents) and Oahu (15.69 cents). Oahu comes in lowest because it has the highest concentration of people and easiest methods of delivery, as opposed to the Big Island, which has vast rural areas and a relatively small population that's more spread out.

Maui County is served by Maui Electric Company (MECO); Hawaii County by Hawaii Electric Light Company (HELCO); and Oahu by Hawaiian Electric Company (HECO). Kauai's electric company is an electric cooperative.

No matter your location, if you compare your electric bill with that of your neighbor's, you shouldn't be surprised if the total amounts vary considerably. Even households with identical square footage and the same number of family members will differ in the amount of energy used each month. From how you heat your water to the type of appliances you use and your commitment to energy efficiency, the result will always be reflected in your utility bill.

You can lower your monthly electrical bill substantially by doing simple things such as purchasing energy-efficient appliances, turning off lights and electrical equipment in unoccupied rooms, and avoiding phantom loads from electronic devices left in continual standby mode.

THE COLD TRUTH ABOUT REFRIGERATORS AND FREEZERS

Your neighbor has an old freezer he's giving away, and it's just the thing for storing those extra couple of pounds of steak and fish. Is this an offer you can refuse?

Yes! Not only should you refuse, you should stay far, far away from those old freezers and fridges. They are some of the biggest energy guzzlers around and belong at the dump, not in your home. Here's why: to run a 20-cubic-foot frostless side-by-side refrigerator manufactured before 1980, you could end up paying close to $45 a month in electricity. That's $540 a year just to store that extra stash of food! Compare that to the $21 a month it takes to run a high-efficiency model of the same size and the choice is obvious.

Today's refrigerators and freezers are much more efficient

than those of yesteryear. Federal efficiency standards first took effect in 1993, followed by even stricter standards in 2001. Full-size Energy Star-qualified refrigerators use up to 20 percent less electricity than conventional refrigerators, so it pays to shop around. Read the Energy Guide labels to compare energy costs.

Consider this: a 16-cubic-foot refrigerator/freezer with the freezer on top manufactured before 1980 could cost you up to $27 a month in electricity to run. Manufactured after 1980, it drops to $21, and after 2001, down to $7.05. An Energy Star model manufactured after 2001 averages just $5.10 per month to run.

Depending on the style and brand you select, there are even many variations in the amount of energy a unit will use. Side-by-side refrigerator/freezers use more energy than same-sized models with the freezer on top. Automatic icemakers and cold-water dispensers will increase the unit's energy consumption by 10 to 20 percent.

If you think you need a second refrigerator, it's generally less expensive to operate one large fridge as opposed to two smaller ones, especially if the second fridge is an older model. If you're just looking to keep some extra six-packs cold, consider buying a small Energy Star model instead.

THE NEW AGE OF ENERGY SUCKERS

A plasma high-definition TV uses twice as much electricity than a regular tube TV! A standard 34-inch color TV might cost $7 a month in electricity, while a 50-inch plasma high-definition TV averages more than $14 a month in energy use (based on $.15 per kWh).

There are many new electronic devices that need electricity even when not in use. Televisions and VCRs in continuous standby mode suck up about 1,000 kilowatt-hours a year per household. Chargers for battery-operated devices like cell phones, iPods and cordless phones waste at least half the energy they need while plugged in. Big-screen televisions also draw a lot of energy when turned off, mostly because of the continuously running satellite and cable boxes. Cable or DSL modems are also likely to be left on 24/7 and use equal amounts of energy to run in active and standby modes.

According to the U.S. Environmental Protection Agency, computers, home entertainment systems and other electronic devices consume about four percent of today's average household energy bill. A whopping 75 percent of the electricity used for home electronics is consumed when the units are turned off and in standby mode.

To reduce these so-called "phantom loads," unplug devices like cell phone chargers when not in use, or use a power strip or wall switch to conveniently turn off computers and chargers.

As new standards begin to be implemented for electronics, look for the energy-rated products as they appear on the market.

CHILL OUT ON AIR CONDITIONER USE

It costs between 20 and 40 cents per hour to run a window air conditioner. A typical central AC system costs up to $1.00 per hour to run. Things can add up quickly. For the average-sized Hawaii home, that's about $1,400 a year for air conditioning.

Obviously, the best way to save on air conditioning is not to have it in your home at all. Natural ventilation, cool roofs, tinted windows and attic vents go a long way toward keeping homes cool. That said, the cost of air conditioning can be minimized if you opt for a high-performance unit and run it efficiently.

When shopping for an air conditioner, examine the energy-efficiency ratings closely. For central air conditioners, you'll want a SEER (seasonal energy-efficiency ratio) rating of 13 or higher. For room air conditioners, the EER (energy-efficiency ratio) rating should be 10 or higher.

Although a high-efficiency unit will cost more, it will pay for itself over the long run in a hot climate like Hawaii. Energy Star-rated room air conditioners use at least 10 percent less energy than conventional air conditioners.

To save on your utility bill, operate your air conditioner only when you're home. Keep your windows closed when the air conditioning is on, and set the thermostat at the warmest comfortable setting. You can install a programmable thermostat so that the air conditioner runs only at times when you need it, programming it to come on a half-hour before you get home from work, for example.

Look for the ENERGY STAR® label when purchasing appliances. These are the most energy-efficient units on the market and will save you money in the long run. Read the Energy Guide labels to compare energy costs.

MORE ENERGY-SAVING TIPS

• USE COMPACT FLORESCENT LIGHTS. THEY USE 75-PERCENT LESS ENERGY THAN STANDARD INCANDESCENT BULBS. PLUS THEY ARE COOLER AND LAST 10 TIMES LONGER. CHANGING ONE 100-WATT BULB TO THE FLORESCENT EQUIVALENT COULD SAVE MORE THAN $16 A YEAR.

• REPAIR LEAKING HOT WATER FAUCETS.

• TURN OFF LIGHTS AND ELECTRICAL EQUIPMENT WHEN THEY'RE NOT IN USE.

• USE COLD WATER FOR LAUNDRY AND TRY TO DO FULL LOADS ONLY. IN HAWAII, "COLD" WATER IS USUALLY ABOUT ROOM TEMPERATURE.

• REPLACE THAT ELECTRIC HOT WATER HEATER WITH SOLAR HEATING, A HEAT PUMP OR AN ON-DEMAND HOT WATER HEATER THAT USES PROPANE.

• RUN THE DISHWASHER ONLY WHEN THERE IS A FULL LOAD.

• USE THE AIR-DRYER CYCLE ON YOUR DISHWASHER TO SAVE ENERGY.

• BUY AN ENERGY STAR-QUALIFIED TELEVISION. IT WILL USE 25-PERCENT LESS ELECTRICITY THAN A STANDARD TV.

• SHORTENING YOUR SHOWER TIMES BY TWO MINUTES COULD SAVE UP TO $230 PER YEAR.

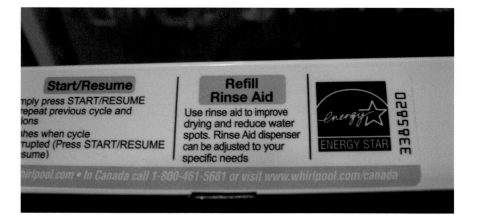

On-Demand Hot Water Heaters

The Paloma brand of on-demand hot water heaters has been a mainstay in the Islands for decades. Hooked to your propane supply, an on-demand hot water heater will save you almost half the cost in monthly utility costs over an electric hot water heater.

When it comes to heating water for the home, on-demand hot water heaters have been hot in Hawaii for decades. Fueled by propane, this nifty little appliance takes up less space than the standard hot water heater. Not only is it more cost effective to operate than an electric or natural gas hot water heater, it is a much faster way to heat water. That's because an on-demand hot water heater (also called "tankless" or "instantaneous") gives you hot water only when you need it, as opposed to the big tank that sits there holding hot water at all times whether it's being used or not.

The savings are significant. Whereas an electric hot water heater might cost $58.80 in electricity for a month, a propane heater averages substantially less energy: $31.20 will pay for a month's propane-heated water for a family of four, according to 2005 estimates by The Gas Company.

On-demand means just that. The water is heated only when the hot water is being used. Good water pressure is key. If you're on water catchment, you might need to install a pressure pump to compensate for the forces of gravity that can impair water pressure.

IT'S A TANKLESS JOB....

Paloma

The Japanese-manufactured Paloma has been used in Hawaii for more than 20 years and is still going strong. There are two models, the PH6 and the PH12, priced between $650 and $1,079 respectively. Homeowners can install and attach them to any size propane tank or cylinder. The parts are easy to replace and repairs are easy to make.

Rinnai

The Rinnai Continuum brand of on-demand hot water heater produces triple the amount of hot water the Paloma does, generating about eight and a half gallons of hot water a minute versus the Paloma's three gallons a minute. The Rinnai is good for extra-large households where there might be two showers going at once along with laundry and the dishes.

Homeowners are restricted from installing the Rinnai themselves. Only a licensed contractor can purchase and install one. Both the indoor and outdoor models run about $1,300 each.

Bosch AquaStar

Bosch USA manufactures several models for use in the home. The 125 Series delivers three to four gallons of hot water per minute, while the Bosch 250 allows for two major uses at one time and delivers almost six and a half gallons of hot water per minute. The Model 38 B is a low-volume-demand unit designed for farm use and camping.

Takagi

The T-K2 or T-KD20 models can supply two showers simultaneously with hot water, both delivering up to five gallons of continuous hot water per minute. Takagi tankless water heaters must be purchased from a licensed contractor/plumber. There's a TK Junior that can be installed indoors or outdoors and delivers three and a half gallons per minute. All have temperature remote-control options.

In Hawaii, on-demand hot water heaters typically run on propane. Make sure the valve on your propane cylinder is open all the way. Leaving the valve partially open could inadvertently seal off some of the gas.

Propane

In Hawaii, propane is commonly used for heating water and powering gas appliances. From pools, spas and tiki torches to barbecues, stoves, clothes dryers and hot water heaters, there are many uses for propane in the Islands.

According to The Gas Company, the savings are significant compared to electricity. Typically, a gas hot-water heater will use approximately 11 gallons of propane per month, a gas range two gallons per month and a clothes dryer two gallons per month. For a household of four, the total monthly energy savings of all three appliances combined is about 40 percent as compared to electricity—and even more if you use an on-demand hot water heater.

Most Hawaii residents utilize some amount of propane in their homes. Propane is also used in rural areas off the grid and as a fuel option for power generators and for refrigerators and freezers.

Portable propane cylinders come in sizes ranging from the small barbecue tanks to the large 48-inch-tall cylinders. Keeping multiple cylinders on hand will save you trips to the dispensing station.

GETTING YOUR SUPPLY

There are two types of gas service available from The Gas Company. Utility gas service is rendered through an underground gas piping system and a gas meter to individual homes or businesses. Non-utility gas service involves tanks or cylinders used by individual homes or businesses where utility gas service is not available.

For new residents familiar only with natural gas, propane involves a bit of education.

Tanks

Your propane can be stored in a large tank or in portable cylinders connected to the gas-supply piping attached to the target appliances. The horizontal tanks come in several different sizes: 124, 288 or 499 gallons and up. To refill a horizontal tank, The Gas Company will come to your house with their big truck and hook into the tank. When your existing propane falls below the 30-percent mark on the gauge, it's time to call The Gas Company to schedule a delivery.

If you are a full-time resident, The Gas Company can put you on a regular service schedule based on your average amount of usage, which is determined after the first two fills. If you fall out of that range occasionally, the delivery schedule is automatically adjusted to minimize interruption of gas service. If your usage is inconsistent from month to month, you will be required to monitor your own propane levels and to call in delivery requests.

Any propane tank larger than 124 gallons needs to be set back a minimum of 10 feet from the house and be accessible for refilling. It's okay to have the 124-gallon tank next to the house as long as it's not located underneath the house, the lanai or an overhang. The tank should not sit directly on the ground but preferably on cement blocks.

If you live on a four-wheel-drive road, The Gas Company won't be able to provide filling services. Portable cylinders are your next option.

Portable Cylinders

Portable cylinders come in sizes ranging from the small 20-pound barbecue tanks to the 100-pound, 48-inch-tall cylinders. When using cylinders, homeowners must personally haul them to the nearest dispensing station for refilling. This requires removing the cylinder from your system, lugging it to the station and back, and then reattaching it to the system.

Once you've reconnected the cylinder, be sure to open its valve all the way. You will not save on propane with a partially opened valve, nor is it any less flammable or dangerous. In fact, leaving the valve partially open could present a problem because you might inadvertently seal off some of the gas.

Users must personally haul their portable cylinders to their local dispensing station for refilling. A certified propane professional will fill the cylinders for you.

It's no fun to run out of propane in the middle of taking a hot shower or cooking an elaborate meal. If you're relying on portable cylinders, have an extra cylinder or two on hand. You can also attach multiple cylinders to your system so when you run out of propane in one you can manually switch to the other. An automatic switchover valve can also be installed.

SAFETY FIRST

Homeowners will sometimes try to do their own installation, but it's best to hire a licensed and experienced professional. Tanks should be placed out in the open, not under the structure, because if ever there is a leak, gas can accumulate under a building.

The distinctive odor of propane is there for one reason: to alert you to leaks. Many times, the smell of propane is indicative of an aging appliance where the burners are clogged or the gas ports have become enlarged from over-cleaning. To check for leaks, brush a solution of dishwashing liquid and water on the joints, valve stems and connections around the cylinder. If there is a leak, bubbles will form from the pressure. A leak test should be done every time you reconnect the cylinders.

If you smell the consistent strong odor of propane inside or outside your house, call The Gas Company immediately. They will waste no time in coming to inspect.

If your house is being fumigated for termites, it's essential that your gas is shut off and that there aren't any appliances still operating on pilot.

WHERE DOES IT COME FROM?

Propane is a high-grade byproduct of refined petroleum; therefore, the price of propane can be, but is not always, affected by the price of crude oil. When the cost of crude oil goes up, it could have a significant bearing on the cost of propane.

Propane is a liquefied petroleum gas that is non-toxic, colorless, and, until the identifying odorant is added, odorless. When contained in a cylinder or tank, propane exists as a liquid stored under its own pressure. Propane is utilized and burned as a vapor in the majority of applications. When the vapor is released from the container, it becomes a clean-burning gas.

Ninety percent of the U.S. propane supply is manufactured domestically. Most of Hawaii's propane supply comes from two refineries on Oahu. Propane is also available from foreign sources outside the U.S. Although natural gas is more economical than propane because it doesn't need to be manufactured, Hawaii does not have significant-enough reserves of natural gas for it to be stored and utilized.

When the gauge on your horizontal tank nears the 30-percent mark, it's time to call The Gas Company for refilling. If you are a full-time resident, The Gas Company can put you on a regular delivery schedule based on your average amount of usage.

Rainwater Catchment

In the state of Hawaii, there are an estimated 60,000 people who depend on collecting rainwater for their household water needs. While a majority of residents on catchment live in rural areas on the Big Island, there are many places across the state where water catchment has been a way of life for generations.

On Oahu, the biggest concentration of households on catchment is in the Tantalus area mauka of Punchbowl. On Maui, it's the Haiku area.

No matter where you live in Hawaii, there are no government agencies that regulate or oversee the safety of catchment water systems. It is up the individual homeowner to understand exactly what is involved in maintaining rainwater for bathing, washing, flushing, laundry, irrigation and, in some cases, drinking.

COLLECTING WATER

Catching rainwater begins on the roof. In Hawaii, the galvanized metal roof is the norm for most homes on catchment. Concrete and terra cotta tiles can also be utilized. Of course, any roofing material that might contain lead, petroleum or fungicide shouldn't be used for catching water—the toxins will leach right into your water supply. If you live in an older home, test the exterior for lead-based paint. Simple test kits are available at local hardware stores.

Before building a new home that will be on catchment, consider the fact that a roof with a relatively low pitch will bring the most rainwater into your tank. With a brand-new roof, it's a good idea to let it rain a few times before connecting the system to flush away any construction particles from the roof.

Gutters made of PVC or plastic, installed in a continuous downward slope leading to the tank, are best for catchment systems. Ideally, the downspout should be angled in such a way that the water completely drains out of it, rather than the typical vertical downspout that is then piped across the ground and up into the tank in a U shape, which might leave standing water in portions of the pipe.

Decaying leaves and twigs will affect the color and clarity of your water and provide nutrients for bacteria to grow in. Gutters should be kept free of debris and organic material.

Screening your gutters will help keep the system clear of debris, but it's a high-maintenance situation that requires a ladder. For easier access, locate screens on pipes or downspouts within reach.

An automatic first-flush diverter is a device that diverts the initial flow of water away from the tank when rain starts to fall. This will wash away many of the contaminants—like bird droppings, molds, dust and volcanic particles—that may have accumulated on the roof since the last rain, and keep them from entering your tank.

Old-style redwood catchment tanks are still in use in some rural areas of Hawaii. Rainwater is collected from the roof of the house and piped into the tank.

TANKS A LOT...

In the old days, redwood tanks were the standard for catching water in Hawaii. Then when wood became too expensive, portable swimming pool tanks came into vogue. While many older homes still have the swimming pool tanks in use today, circular corrugated metal tanks are now the norm.

If you have purchased an old home with a redwood tank, check to make sure it hasn't been painted on the inside. If it has, have the water analyzed for lead. Swimming pool tank liners can be a problem because they might contain toxins designed to prevent fungal growth in a pool. Therefore, if you purchase a swimming pool tank, you should buy a liner approved by the Food and Drug Administration for catching water, even if you're not drinking the water.

Mesh covers on metal tanks should be positioned above the waterline. Take whatever measures you can to prevent the mesh cover from sagging in the water.

Corrugated metal tanks are relatively inexpensive compared to other styles of tank. Make sure you use only the liners that are FDA approved.

Concrete tanks are more expensive than metal and might be susceptible to cracking in the event of an earthquake. Ferroconcrete tanks are a lot more flexible than the old cement tanks and will hold up well.

The benefit of a concrete tank is that the calcium in the cement helps to reduce the acid content of acid rain. Additionally, concrete tanks are strong enough to support a solid cover and sometimes can be concealed in the design of the house.

Although the ideal covering for a tank is a solid cover, this can be very expensive. Covers are often too heavy for most metal tanks to support, unless the tank is designed for one. Most homeowners opt for mesh covers instead, but the problem with these is that contaminants can still enter your tank through the mesh. Sunlight can also filter through, promoting algae. Additionally, mesh covers tend to sag into the water when the tank is full, creating a "pond" that attracts birds, mosquitoes and debris. Take whatever measures you can to prevent your mesh cover from sagging into the water.

If you can afford it, the best option is either a solid-covered concrete tank, a food-grade polyethylene tank or a food-grade fiberglass tank. These provide the best protection against contamination, animals and debris.

PUMP IT UP: HERE'S HOW IT WORKS

A pump system for catchment includes the pump, a pressure tank, check valves and a pressure switch. The system draws water from the tank, pressurizes it, and stores it in the pressure tank until needed. Water is delivered when you first open the faucet, then the pump switch activates the pump to deliver more water from the tank. For best performance, the pump should be located at the same level as the water storage tank. Installing a larger pressure tank will also help the pump perform at its optimum.

If you notice a drop in water pressure, the first thing to check is the filter. It's possible for a dirty filter to completely block the flow of water. To keep your system clean and operating efficiently, the filter should be changed once a month.

If your pH level is too low, it means the water is too acidic from acid rain. A little baking soda added to the water will help solve the problem.

BUT CAN I DRINK IT?: WATER TREATMENT METHODS

A typical family of four on catchment might use about 200 gallons of water a day, 80 gallons of which might be used for flushing and 65 gallons for bathing.

A filter system can include everything from UV light to an absolute 1-micron filter. Check your filter regularly to ensure that your system is clean and operating efficiently.

Because your catchment water comes in contact with your dishes and with your skin through bathing, hand washing, showers and other means, it must be treated. Chlorine is the number-one recommended chemical product for treating catchment water because it kills a lot of the bad stuff, including leptospira bacteria, which is found in the urine of mammals.

Leptospira is highly prevalent in Hawaii and is usually contracted through contact with the soft mucus membranes and through skin cuts. Because there is a good chance that an occasional (or not-so-occasional) rat will run across your roof, it's imperative that you treat your catchment water with chlorine. You need to have 1 part per million dilution of chlorine in your water at all times, obtained by adding two ounces of unscented household bleach (six-percent strength) per 1,000 gallons of water monthly or biweekly depending on the frequency of rainfall.

To achieve even distribution, mix the chlorine in a bucket of water before adding it the tank, then stir the water, if you are able, with a length of PVC pipe or a paddle. Try not to pour the chlorine solution next to the pipe that goes into the house because all the chlorine could be pulled into the pipe before it's mixed in the tank.

Chlorine will also kill bacteria, fungi and viruses, but chlorine treatment alone does not reduce risks for some organisms, such as the ones that cause *Giardia* or *Cryptosporidium*.

The Hawaii Department of Health does not recommend the drinking of catchment water, but there are a number of residents who successfully drink their catchment water and swear by its purity. The use of an absolute 1-micron filter is recommended, but the best option would be an ultraviolet light (Class A), which will kill most, but not all, pathogens. It will not kill *Toxoplasma gondii*, for example, but if you have a solid cover and no cats on the roof, you shouldn't have a problem.

Bottled water can be kept on hand for brushing teeth, cleaning vegetables and for your pet's drinking water as well. Many residents on catchment fetch their drinking and cooking water from public spigots. When the tank gets low, outside sources of water can be trucked in for a fee. Be sure your water hauler is from a reputable company.

If you decide you want to use your catchment water for drinking, do your research. Not all filters do what they are touted to do. For more information about water testing and water catchment, contact the College of Tropical Agriculture and Human Resources Cooperative Extension Office in Hilo at (808) 981-5199. The office has published a highly informative 52-page booklet about catching rainwater in Hawaii and will send one to you upon request.

Solar Electric

There are hundreds of farms and homes in the state of Hawaii equipped with solar-electric systems that generate the bare basics of electricity. This coffee farm in Captain Cook operates entirely off the grid.

Thinking of going solar for your home?
Solar-electric power can be as simple as a garden light or attic fan or as comprehensive as a complete photovoltaic (PV) system that meets all your electrical requirements—assuming you have the funds to install one.

There are hundreds of homes and farms in the state of Hawaii, especially in rural areas, equipped with solar-electric systems that can generate the bare basics of electricity. Some homes are interactive with the utility grid, exporting surplus electricity to the distribution network, while other residents are completely self-reliant, generating and storing their own power for everything from outbuildings, sheds and farm equipment to all of their household needs.

If the idea of not being able to plug in a microwave oven, hair dryer or toaster sounds too primitive for you, then you won't be happy with a small solar setup for long. Conversely, if you have a large home, you could spend anywhere from $30,000 to $100,000 to cover your entire electrical needs with solar. As pricey as that sounds, it's still a lot cheaper than using electricity from the power company if you live a distance from the nearest utility line and want to extend the utility to your property—which would cost at least $3,500 per pole. Considering poles are installed 200 to 250 feet apart, most people would opt to go all the way with solar and generate their own power.

POWER SHIFT—SUBTRACT DOLLARS WITH NET METERING

There is a way to combine your self-generated electricity with that of ye olde reliable utility company. It's called net energy metering, and it's just now starting to catch on with Hawaii residents.

With net energy metering, you connect your qualified renewable energy system to the utility grid, allowing it to feed electricity into the grid when you have a surplus or run on the utility's power when you have a deficit. The utility replaces, at no charge to the customer, its standard meter with an electric one that records the amount of surplus electricity your system exports to the utility. Whatever you generate yourself is used to meet your electricity needs and any extra is exported to the utility and credited to your account. Electricity is most often exported when you're not using it—during the day when you're at work, for example.

Then on a cloudy day, at night, or when more electricity is being used than is being generated, you tap into the utility company's supply, and the meter records the amount of electricity you're using beyond what your PV system generates.

Essentially, you usually end up generating all the power that you use, even though you're washing it through the utility. Net energy metering allows you to get more value from the electricity you generate because you are offsetting your purchase of electricity from your utility against excess electricity produced by your

Photovoltaic panels capture the sun's energy and change it to DC electricity, to be converted to 120-volt AC current by the system's inverter. You can spend between $30,000 and $100,000 to cover your entire electrical needs with solar.

renewable system at the retail rate. Excess credits may be carried forward to the next month, for up to 12 months.

SIGN ME UP...

To participate, you must sign up with your electric company if your system is connected to the utility. There is no charge to sign up for net metering with HECO, HELCO and MECO (Kauai has a small fee), but when you enter into a customer agreement with the utility, you'll need to hire a licensed electrical contractor as required by Hawaii state law. All Hawaii counties require electrical permits be issued before the system installation begins.

Net metering applies to solar and other types of renewable systems, like wind power, that generate electricity, but it does not apply to solar thermal. Since a solar hot-water heating system does not produce electricity, it does not feed electricity back into the grid and therefore would not qualify for net energy metering.

TAX INCENTIVES...OR LACK THEREOF

In Hawaii, residents who install a photovoltaic system are eligible for a $5,000 state tax credit or 35 percent of the cost of the system, whichever is less. In comparison to the percentage residents can save on solar hot water heating, this is not as good a deal, considering the high cost of PV systems. By contrast, if a business wants to install photovoltaics or other alternative energy systems, it can obtain credits of 35 percent of the cost—up to a maximum of $500,000.

Under the federal Energy Policy Act of 2005, you can also be eligible for a 30-percent federal tax credit on the cost of a qualified PV system, installed from January 1, 2006 through December 31, 2008, up to a maximum tax credit limitation of $2,000. Consult with your tax advisor on how to calculate this latest credit.

The Hawaii State Legislature recently passed a landmark bill, signed into law by the Governor, that requires homeowner and condo associations to adapt guidelines to facilitate the installation of solar systems, both solar electric or thermal (hot water), and to allow for the installation of solar systems including solar hot-water heating for single-family dwellings and townhomes. This bill will surely open the residential market so that more homeowners can install solar systems in places where they were once prohibited (because the panels were considered unsightly, for instance).

SAY WATT?

Do you have to be a scientist to deal with your solar system, calculating down to the last watt how much energy you need on a daily basis? Fortunately, no—the system's inverter does most of the work. You just need to do the actual calculations before the system is installed to make sure that your PV system is sufficient to handle your loads.

So how does it all work? A stand-alone solar electric system consists of four basic parts: photovoltaic panels, charge controller, batteries and inverter. The PV panel is made of semi-conductor cells, usually silicon, that capture the sun's energy and change it to DC electricity. The electricity is then fed to the charge controller, which prevents overcharging by feeding into the batteries at a regulated rate. Electricity is stored in the batteries until needed, then sent to an inverter that converts the DC into 120-volt AC current. This output can be wired into your standard circuit breaker box.

The power you draw depends on how much power you have in your batteries and the size of your inverter. A 4-kilowatt inverter will allow you to run 4,000 watts worth of appliances at once, for example. The average household might use at least 15,000 watts a day.

The number of panels and your energy-conservation practices are what make the difference. For a basic small system, you need a minimum of four panels. Panels come in different sizes and watt ratings such as 75-, 85-, 125-, 160- and 175-watt. With six 175-watt panels and four-and-a-half hours of good sun, you'll get about 1,000 watts per hour.

Technological advances are making it possible to generate even more sun power all day long. The Mauna Lani Resort installed the Solar Electric PowerTracker, in which PV panels are tilted toward the sun and move throughout the day to continuously face the light, increasing the electrical energy output by 35 percent.

WHEN SUNNY GETS BLUE

Unfortunately, these days panels are in big demand and are hard to come by. Germany, Japan and Australia are actively acquiring most of the world's panels. In Hawaii, as in other parts of the country, you have to get on a waiting list with your solar supplier, as most panels are on back order. In the meantime, keep hoping that new technological innovations in the solar marketplace will come along, as well as better Hawaii tax incentives for the residents who generate their own power with solar electricity.

Electricity captured from the sun is stored in batteries until needed. A charge controller is needed to prevent overcharging while an inverter converts the DC electricity to AC current.

Solar Hot Water

Hawaii is the number-one state in the nation for solar hot water usage. There are still tax and utility incentives available for residents who switch to solar.

Hawaii homeowners can reap big savings when using the sun to heat water. How much savings, you ask? Thousands of dollars!

Suppose you pay $4,700 for your new solar hot-water system, including installation. If you apply the utility rebate of up to $1,000 (for qualifying systems) and then take advantage of the 35-percent Hawaii State tax credit and the 30-percent federal tax credit, you could slice that initial purchase price by more than half—for a final cost of $1,683.50.

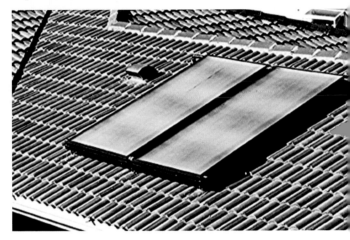

Then after just a few short years of heating water with the sun for free, you'll have matched that price in energy savings. The savings will continue for the life of the system, at least another 15 years or more.

In short, solar is a better investment than putting the same amount of money into the stock market.

HOT SAVINGS

For most households, heating water can account for the biggest part of the energy bill, sometimes more than half the total. The truth is, electric hot water heaters are a big waste of money. A solar water-heating system, on the other hand, can save the average homeowner 30 to 50 percent on their monthly utility bill.

Not only does solar water heating save the homeowner money each month, it's also good for the environment. It is estimated that for every solar water-heating system installed in Hawaii, almost five and a half barrels (277 gallons) of oil are saved per year. Multiply that by the tens of thousands of Hawaii residents on solar, and the result is helping to make Hawaii less dependent on imported sources of energy.

Solar systems heat up to 95 percent of your water without added energy input. Most systems will last for 20 years, are relatively low maintenance and will provide the highest potential savings over the life of the system compared to other water heating technologies. These benefits, along with tax incentives, utility rebates and year-round sunshine, are just some of the reasons why Hawaii is the state ranked number-one in the nation for solar hot water usage.

You can identify solar hot water panels by the water pipes that are attached to the system. Pictured above is an active system, which relies on an electrical pump to circulate water between the solar collectors and the storage tank.

Any dealer that installs a system must have a contractor's solar specialty license. To take advantage of utility rebates, you must choose from the utility company's list of pre-screened, qualified contractors.

INCENTIVES

- **State Tax Credit:** As of July 2006, the Hawaii State Solar Water heating Tax Credit is 35 percent or $2,250 for single-family homes or townhomes, whichever is less. The credit can be claimed only if you owe taxes, and can be carried forward to future years until used.

- **Federal Tax Credit:** Homeowners can now earn a tax credit of up to 30 percent of the cost of installing a solar hot-water system, up to $2,000, as long as it is certified by the Solar Rating and Certification Corporation (SRCC). This credit applies to systems installed after January 1, 2006 through December 31, 2008.

- **Utility Rebates:** Hawaiian Electric Company (HECO), Maui Electric Company (MECO), and Hawaii Electric Light Company (HELCO) offer varying rebates that range from $750 to $1,000. Kauai Island Utility Cooperative's rebate level is fixed at $800.

  To be eligible for the rebate, you must be a customer of the local electric utility and have previously heated your water with electricity. If you're converting from gas to solar, you will not qualify. To take advantage of the utility rebate, you'll need to choose from the utility company's list of pre-screened, qualified contractors.

- **Mortgage Benefits:** When you finance your solar system as part of the mortgage, you save money from the moment you walk in the door, because the mortgage payment attributable to the solar is less than what you'll be paying in utility. Additionally, your interest rates are usually lower than on a short-term loan, and closing costs may be reduced, especially when you qualify for Energy Efficient Mortgages through the U.S. EPA's "Energy Star Homes" program.

SOAK UP THE SUN

There are two kinds of solar water-heating systems. The active (forced-circulation) system uses pumps to circulate water. The passive (thermosiphon) system uses natural convection to keep the water flowing.

Often resembling a partially rolled-up sleeping bag on the roof, a passive system needs no mechanical pump or electricity. The storage tank is located higher than the collector panels where the water is heated. Water slowly moves upward into the tank as it heats up, and the cooler water descends to replace it.

With an active system, an electrical pump (either AC or DC) circulates the water between the solar collectors and the storage tank. With an AC pump, temperature sensors and a differential controller turn the pump on and off repeatedly during the day, depending on the amount of heat generated by the sun. The DC pump is powered by a small photovoltaic panel.

Which type of system you choose depends on your needs. When considering a system, it pays to shop around. There are lots of qualified installers and companies to choose from. Prices and system sizes vary.

Any dealer that installs your system must have a contractor's solar specialty license. If your dealer doesn't do installations, be sure to check out the credentials of the installer you hire. You can also use a licensed plumbing contractor and a licensed electrician to do the plumbing and the electrical.

MAINTENANCE

A solar water-heating system will heat water during the day and store the heated water in the tank for day and night usage. If there are successive days of cloudy skies, hot water is usually provided by electric backup. Propane for backup is not recommended unless you live off the grid.

Most water heater tanks are warranted for five years, and most solar water-heating collectors are warranted for 10 years. Some signs that your system may not be performing at optimum capacity include: loss of hot water at night, continual running of the pump, water that is too hot or too cold, and, of course, no hot water at all.

You can pay for annual maintenance, or you can do it yourself. Just remember to read all warning labels before attempting any diagnosis or repair, as you could be dealing with scalding hot water or the possibility of electric shock.

There are solar hot water systems designed to heat swimming pools. (above). The solar panels can be draped on the roof (pictured below) or placed anywhere outside the home.

Maintenance basics include flushing your storage tank to rid it of debris, checking for leaks, cleaning the collector glass and making sure that the mounting structures are not corroded. To clean the glass, use mild soapy water on a cool day when the glass is not hot.

The anode rod is inside the tank to protect it from corrosion. It should be replaced every five years—more often if your water temperature runs between 130 and 150 degrees. A professional is usually required for the job because it takes a special wrench to remove it.

AIN'T NO SUNSHINE WHEN SHE'S GONE

If you are going on vacation or will be away for a long period of time, you should make sure that your system doesn't overheat while you're gone. For an active system, change the controller switch from "automatic" to "on" before you go on your trip. This allows the pump to run constantly and prevents overheating.

Some people with passive systems conceal the collectors with a shading screen or tarp. Since there is no way to turn off a passive system, covering up the collectors will prevent the sun from heating the water. But this is also a dead giveaway that nobody is home. ❖

Sometimes resembling a partially rolled-up sleeping bag on the roof, a passive system uses natural convection to keep the water flowing and requires no pump or electricity. Notice that the storage tank is located higher than the collecting panels.

APPLIANCE ENERGY COSTS
2004 Average Energy Cost per kWh per Island:

	Average kWh Usage	Unit of Use	Big Island @ .24
APPLIANCES			
Coffeemaker, 12-cup auto perk	0.17	brew	.04
Dishwasher	1.00	load	.24
Microwave oven, 20 minutes	.50	use	.12
Oven	1.6	hour	.38
Vacuum cleaner	3.25	month	.78
Rice cooker	0.17	use	.04
Toaster oven	0.13	20 min	.03
LAUNDRY/WATER HEATING			
Clothes dryer	3.00	load	.72
Washing machine			
(cold wash/cold rinse)	0.33	load	.08
(warm wash/cold rinse)	2.3	load	.55
(hot wash/hot rinse)	8.3	load	1.99
Water heater, 100 degrees	400	month	96.00
REFRIGERATORS/FREEZERS			
Refrigerator, 16 cu. ft. (manufactured before 1980)	180	month	43.00
Refrigerator, 16 cu. ft. (manufactured after 1980)	140	month	33.60
Refrigerator, 16, cu. ft. (manufactured after 2001)	47	month	11.28
Refrigerator, 16 cu. ft. (Energy Star after 2001)	34	month	8.16
Chest Freezer, 16 cu. ft. (manufactured before 1980)	100	month	24.00
Chest Freezer, 16 cu. ft. (Energy Star)	30	month	7.20

Maui @ .21	Molokai @ .26	Oahu @ .16	Lanai @ .25	Kauai @ .26
.03	.04	.03	.04	.04
.21	.26	.16	.25	.26
.11	.13	.08	.13	.13
.34	.42	.25	.40	.42
.68	.85	.52	.81	.85
.03	.04	.03	.04	.04
.03	.03	.02	.03	.03
.63	.78	.48	.75	.78
.07	.08	.05	.08	.08
.48	.60	.37	.58	.60
1.74	2.16	1.32	2.08	2.16
84.00	104.00	64.00	100.00	104.00
37.80	46.80	28.00	45.00	46.80
29.40	36.49	22.00	35.00	36.49
9.87	12.22	7.50	11.75	12.22
7.14	8.84	5.44	8.50	8.84
21.00	26.00	16.00	25.00	26.00
6.30	7.80	4.80	7.50	7.80

In the state of Hawaii, Oahu has the lowest residential electrical rates of all the islands, averaging 16 cents a kilowatt hour in 2004.

Residents on Molokai and Kauai paid the most—an average of 26 cents per kilowatt hour in 2004.

The next highest in 2004 was Lanai (25), followed by the Big Island (24), and Maui (21).

(These rates do not include monthly taxes and surcharges and are based on estimates by the respective utilities.)

APPLIANCE ENERGY COSTS (continued)
2004 Average Energy Cost per kWh per island:

	Average kWh Usage*	Unit of Use	Big Island @ .24
ENTERTAINMENT			
27-inch video TV (on mode)	32.40	month	7.78
Plasma high definition 50-inch TV	93.60	month	22.46
Video cable box Converter, digital (on mode)	5.76	month	1.38
(standby mode)	13.50	month	3.24
COMFORT			
Swimming pool pump (1 horsepower)	240	month	57.60
Swimming pool sweep (3/4 horsepower)	69.75	month	16.74
Ceiling fan	0.40	day	.10
Oscillating fan	0.40	day	.10
Air conditioning** Room and small-split system 18,000 Btu/H (1 Ton)	222.6	month[1]	53.52
Central and large-split system 36,000 Btu/H (3 Ton)	816	month[2]	195.84
Portable 10,000 Btu/H	158.40	month[2]	38

* A kilowatthour (kWh) is equal to one 100-watt bulb operating for 10 hours
** Consumption depends on area to be cooled, insulation condition and hours used.
1 4 hr/day, compressor "on"
2 8 hr/day, compressor "on"

Maui @ .21	Molokai @ .26	Oahu @ .16	Lanai @ .25	Kauai @ .26
6.80	8.42	5.20	8.10	8.42
19.66	23.34	14.97	23.40	23.34
1.21	1.50	.92	1.44	1.50
2.84	3.51	2.16	3.38	3.51
50.40	62.40	38.40	60.00	62.40
14.65	18.14	11.16	17.44	18.14
.08	.10	.06	.10	.10
.08	.10	.06	.10	.10
46.74	57.87	35.62	55.65	57.87
171.36	212.16	130.56	204	212.16
33.26	41.18	25.34	39.60	41.18

Finishing Touches

Decorative Concrete

The old gray mare, she ain't what she used to be—gray as in concrete, that is.

Always a bit drab and often downright unsightly, conventional gray concrete has undergone a total transformation in the home industry. As many homeowners in Hawaii are discovering, the use of decorative concrete treatments can turn those cold, gray slabs into unique and stylish additions, replicating the beauty of natural stone or the opulence of inlays at half the cost of traditional masonry.

With looks ranging from cobblestone, tile, granite and slate to flagstone, brick, wood, lava rock and pahoehoe, decorative concrete provides a variety of realistic alternatives for floors, walkways, entryways, bathrooms, pool decks, driveways and patios. What's more, it can actually be stronger that the natural materials and should hold up for years, even in high-traffic areas.

And you don't even need to tear out your old concrete to install it.

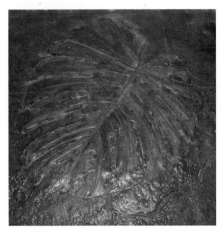

MAKING AN IMPRESSION

In the world of decorative concrete, three basic techniques are used: stamping/stenciling, staining and overlay. The design choices are limited only by your imagination and, more importantly, the workmanship and skill of your concrete contractor.

Not long ago, the choice of products in Hawaii was limited. Today, the availability of new products and applications has brought the general price of decorative concrete treatments down considerably. A variety of manufacturer's systems are used. Individual contractors usually stick with one or two preferred product lines. Increte Systems, L.M. Scofield and Elite Crete are just some of the systems widely in use.

Stamped Concrete

A child's handprint in wet cement might well have been the humble inspiration for modern imprinted-concrete technology. Today, pattern stamping involves creating elaborate three-dimensional patterns in newly poured colored concrete or in an overlay on top of existing concrete. Special stamping tools are used, typically rubber mats with protruding designs that are pressed onto the surface to duplicate the look and texture of natural materials

Kiln-dried river gravel (opposite) is mixed with a custom-blended epoxy resin that can be applied to concrete and other surfaces for a permanent bond. The product, Futura Stone, is made to withstand heavy traffic including vehicular, and is ideal for driveways. Concrete stamps (above) bring a touch of nature into the home, such as the monstera print above.

in deep relief patterns.

Flagstone, brick, pavers and cobblestone are just some of the patterns available.

When the stamping is complete, it can be stained to add contrast, color and texture to match any design theme envisioned. The concrete is then sealed to bring out the colors.

Stenciled concrete involves imprinting a pattern into freshly placed concrete with a heavy-duty paper stencil. Large sheets are laid on the surface to produce the look of inlaid brick or stone.

Overlays

For existing concrete that needs a face-lift, polymer cement overlay combines cement, resins and aggregates to form a tougher-than-nails thickness that can range from 1/4 of an inch up to two full inches and more. No matter the thickness, the overlay will hold up to harsh weather conditions and traffic better than conventional concrete. Whether you end up with a slick finish or a swirling, textured effect, the result is the look and durability of a brand-new concrete floor.

Even upon close inspection, it's difficult to tell that this "brick" walkway is made entirely of stamped concrete. Flagstone, brick and cobblestone are just some of the patterns available.

To create an overlay, the existing slab must first be degreased and prepared. Then the overlay can be applied several different ways. A "broom" effect can be achieved by pulling a broom across a thin layer of overlay for texture, while a "trowel-down" produces a smooth, slip-resistant surface in any color.

The overlay can also be stamped or stenciled to replicate natural tile, brick, slate, wood planks and more. Overlays can be chemically stained with translucent colors to create an elegant and durable floor.

Acid Stain

To add pizzazz to a dreary driveway, floor or patio, acid stain is an alternative that can be used for both interior and exterior applications. It's very durable if properly applied and then protected with sealer.

Acid stain is not a paint or coating; rather, it is a coloring process that reacts chemically with the concrete and penetrates the surface more deeply than water- or oil-based products. Antique, glazed and Italian marbled effects are among the mottled looks that can be achieved for entryways, bathrooms and interiors. The defining look is earthy, old, warm and weathered. Different shades can be created by mixing and matching colors, or by varying the rate of application.

Not every concrete floor can be acid stained—it depends on the condition of the slab—and the results can never be guaranteed. Old concrete needs to be thoroughly cleaned and any existing paint or sealer completely removed. After the acid stain is applied, the floor must be sealed for protection, which will also add shine and depth.

Don't expect to get an even tone. The beauty of the acid stain is in its varied, marbled look; some areas will be darker than others. Pre-test a small area so you know exactly what you'll end up with.

Various patterns can be scored into the concrete, giving the floor the appearance of cut stone. When more than one acid-stain color is used, the scored lines help delineate the color changes and keep the color from bleeding outside the pattern. The sky is the limit when it comes to creating designs, patterns and works of art on a concrete floor.

Multi-layered acid stains create the unique look of this concrete floor. Hints of green and amber give the surface a textured look and create a blended color finish.

Exterior Paint and Finishes

From mold, termites and humidity to wind, rain and the intense effects of the sun—Hawaii homes are subject to myriad harsh elements that must be considered when selecting the right paint or finish for your exterior.

A good paint job will go a long way toward protecting your home, not to mention adding lasting beauty and appeal to your most valuable asset.

UV rays are the biggest daily enemy to your home's exterior. Notice how easily the Hawaiian sun can ruin paint on cars, turn plastic brittle, or fade the interior of your home—floors, walls, curtains, photographs and artwork. Now think about your home's exterior and its ability to withstand the daily pounding of UV rays searing down on it. Without the protection of a high-grade paint, your wood exterior can easily succumb to rot, warping, termites and carpenter bees, or turn gray with discoloration.

It makes sense to spend the time and money at the beginning rather than wondering what went wrong a year later when "paint failure" sets in—an unwelcome situation that any seasoned painting contractor knows exactly how to prevent.

CHOOSING YOUR PAINT

In Hawaii, good exterior paint can last five to seven years before it needs to be replaced. Cheap paint, on the other hand, will fail within six months—at the most, three years. Paint that costs less than $20 a gallon is considered "cheap paint," while high-end paint is priced at $28 and up. Although it's tempting to save a few bucks on affordable paint, you will spare yourself future expense and aggravation if you spend the extra money up front.

Why is it important to use good paint in Hawaii? For one thing, cheap paint isn't resistant to mildew. You might try fortifying it by adding an anti-mildew agent, but there's no guarantee it will work when combined with cheap paint. In fact, some paints are so poor they can actually grow mildew right in the can. If you see black floating in your paint, you'll know this has occurred.

No matter where you live in Hawaii, use only exterior paint that includes mildewcide, a chemical agent that destroys, retards or prevents the growth of mildew. If you live at a high or wet elevation, it's even more important that you add extra mildewcide to your paint, even if the paint already contains it. Your local paint store will add it for you on request.

Latex is your best bet for exteriors. Opt for the "shine" or "low-luster" finish because those are the easiest surfaces to clean. It is nearly impossible to remove marks, stains and handprints from a flat ("matte") finish, so determine your true maintenance

A good paint job requires a hefty amount of prep work, including the pressure washing (opposite) of eaves and sidings to remove mold, dirt and stains. Choosing the right color paint can be an agonizing decision for the homeowner (above). Try paint-testing your colors outdoors so that you don't end up with a color you'll regret.

threshold instead of going along with what your architect thinks "looks" good.

A LITTLE LOCAL COLOR

Obnoxious Yellow. Putrid Pink. Eyesore Purple. There are literally thousands of hues to choose from, so be sure your color choice doesn't clash with that of your neighbors, or else your neighbors might decide to clash with you.

Certain colors also last better than others against UV. Whites hold up best, and mid-tones also work well. Generally, the lighter the tone, the longer the color will last against UV. Dark blues, greens, purples and reds tend to break down quickly.

Use a color range that complements the permanent aspects of the house like the roof, brickwork and masonry or the colors of your landscaping and gardens.

Painting the exterior of a house is a big job that requires a lot of prep work, patience and expertise. If you want your paint job to last over the long haul, hire a respected licensed painting contractor for the job.

It's also wise to study your color samples outdoors by paint-testing certain areas of the house. Lighter colors can create the illusion that your house is larger and closer to the street, while darker colors might make your house look smaller and more set back on your lot.

If you are going to paint your house yourself but are not entirely sure what to do, hire a licensed painting contractor for a consultation. Better yet, just hire one for the job. Painting the entire exterior of your home is a big endeavor that involves a lot of expertise, labor and prep work.

PREP

If you're determined to DIY, make sure all surfaces are clean and dry before you paint. Paint will not adhere to anything wet, salty, damp, greasy or dirty. It takes time and plenty of elbow grease to prep surfaces, but preparation is the key step to achieving a quality paint application.

A primer coat should be used to prepare the surface for the top coat. You can paint over existing paint as long as the old paint adheres well to the surface. If there is wood or rust exposed, then you need to use the appropriate primer for each surface. If it's a shiny surface, you'll want to rough it up with some sandpaper.

To prep metal surfaces, grind them down with an electric grinder. Treat existing rust with a product called Osphlo, a phosphorus-conversion coating available at marine stores. Brush it on, let it dry, then prime and paint the metal. This won't keep the rust from eventually coming back, but you can slow down the process with good product and paint.

Don't paint over mildew! This is by far the biggest painting mistake you'll ever make. You are simply sandwiching the mildew between layers of paint, and it will keep on growing and coming out. Nobody likes a mildew sandwich, especially on your house.

If you want to spend money on chemicals to kill mildew, there are products available, such as Jomax, which can be mixed with bleach. But experts say water alone and a good scrub job will work just fine. Pressure-washing your exterior is the best way to remove mildew. A pressure wash will remove lots of "stuff" and sufficiently prep your surface for paint. Hire a professional for the job.

STAINS AND CLEAR WOOD FINISHES

There is nothing you can add to a clear wood finish to prevent mold, because any additive will change the color of the finish. In fact, mold likes clear wood finishes, so don't use them if you live in a wet elevation. Additionally, clear wood finishes tend to break down on the coast.

For trim, Sikkens is the best clear wood finish on the market. Used for new construction, Sikkens is pricy at $65 a gallon, but it will hold up well against UV and looks very elegant.

If you decide to use a stain, bear in mind that when it breaks down, you cannot re-stain over it. Stains are transparent; therefore, when you add another coat, it becomes more opaque. Most stains do not work well for exteriors in Hawaii, as they break down in less than two years from the harsh UV. In actuality, paint is your best option for all exteriors.

Natural Materials

This hot tub hale in Kea-lakekua features ohia posts and handrails and a thatched roof made of prime alungalung grass. The opening in the roof allows for star-gazing at night while soaking in the jarrah-wood hot tub.

Picture yourself poolside sipping a Mai Tai beneath the shade of your thatched-roof bamboo tiki hut with banana-weave ceiling panels, your secret hideaway concealed from view by a tropical privacy screen made of rolled reed and ohia posts. All the while, the exotica sounds of Martin Denny are playing on your iPod as you read *The Book of Tiki*.

Now that you're living in Hawaii, why not bring the essence of the tropics to your backyard, lanai or patio? With occasional upkeep, natural materials can last indefinitely and will add a special tropical ambiance to your surroundings.

THATCH ALL, FOLKS

There's nothing more tropical than a thatched roof. For residential purposes, thatch can be utilized as roofing material for pavilions, pool gazebos, garden hales and spas. If you're planning to install it on a large structure, check with your county's building department regarding regulations and permits.

At first glance, all thatch might look the same, but there are significant differences in quality and material. The least expensive option is "elephant grass" thatch, available in panels of varying lengths. It's okay for the short term if you're throwing a party and need some tropical touches or want to add shade to a structure. But it is highly flammable, can be messy and will pick up mold easily.

Hemmed on one edge, woven palm thatch is more rigid and can be used for roofing, a sham, decor or table skirting. Umbrella thatch comes in one big round piece to drape over a patio umbrella.

The best natural thatch is imported from Indonesia and Mexico, either palm or alungalung grass. Prime alungalung thatch will have no seeds that might attract birds to your roof. If installed at the recommended thickness of 12 inches, it's resistant to pests and will hold up for years even in high winds. Measuring between seven-and-a-half and nine feet long, panels are sewn together with coconut senet (fiber).

Indonesians tie their roofing panels onto the roof frames, but you can use screws or a nail gun. The pitch of the roof you're covering should be fairly steep, as this will help the thatch hold up longer against sun and weather.

An alternative to natural thatch, simulated thatch made of high-grade PVC material has the look and feel of the real thing. The material can be nailed or screwed to the frame and is fire resistant and highly durable even in windy conditions. It's expensive, though—up to $16 a square foot.

Nothing says casual, island living better than bamboo and thatch furniture, offering a shady spot for afternoon cocktails and informal meals.

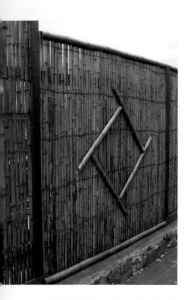

Modular tropical-style fences and gates can be protected with an annual coat of Sikkens marine-grade stain in a butternut color. Fencing will hold up over the long haul if you know how to maintain it.

TROPICAL FENCING

Flexible, lightweight tropical-style fencing comes in a variety of materials—from bamboo, willow twig, branch and brush, to dragon grass, bamboo peel, rattan and reed. In Hawaii, rolled reed is frequently used to make privacy screens, gates and fence paneling. It also makes a great shade covering for the lanai because it allows some light to shine through while providing shade. Standard rolled reed is tied together with regular tie wire that can rust. Look for the superior product that features plastic-coated wire, stainless steel or copper.

Modular outdoor fences and gates made of bamboo are made in a variety of designs and sizes featuring vertical or horizontal lattices, solid panels, or diamond or triangle shapes. Posts with pegs can be installed with each panel. There are many ways to set a bamboo post into the ground, including with cement and rebar.

TIKI HUTS

The tiki trend, which began in California in the '50s, continues to captivate. With a tiki hut or tiki bar beside your pool, it's easy to transform your backyard into a tropical resort. You can order kits online or find them at various wholesalers throughout the Islands.

Characterized by bamboo frames and thatched roofs, tiki structures can run the gamut from a simple porch swing with thatched awning to a tiki bar for your lanai. Tiki huts come in a variety of prices ranges and sizes, great for luaus, seating areas or spa coverings.

Easy to assemble, tiki huts are strong enough to withstand heavy rains, intense sun and strong wind. Some kits even come with ceiling fans, bar sinks, electrical receptacles and lights. And don't forget the cocktail shaker!

CAN-DO BAMBOO

Most of the bamboo available in Hawaii doesn't come from Hawaii at all, but from places like Thailand, Vietnam, China or the Philippines.

Bamboo poles present unlimited ideas for use. You can make simple curtain rods and towel racks or use them for trim, stakes and fencing. Bamboo is often fashioned into conduits to conceal ugly pipes and wiring. It is also strong enough for heavy-duty structural applications like trellises, arbors and gazebos. Pre-fabricated bamboo gazebos are simple to install and will last a lifetime.

The largest-sized bamboo pole, called "tre gei," measures five inches in diameter and up, while "tam vong" bamboo averages two inches around. Comparable to maple or oak in structural integrity, tre gei and tam vong are the strongest of all bamboo and are frequently used to make furniture.

Faux bamboo poles made of PVC can be fashioned to cover up a steel post or I-beam or to sheath a tiki-torch shaft. Imaginative homeowners have created everything from railings and fountains to gutters and downspouts with PVC bamboo.

TIP: Use diluted bleach or peroxide to clean mold off bamboo.

TROPICAL DECORATIVE PANELS

For walls and ceilings, tropical paneling presents a variety of looks and applications. With more than 50 styles to choose from, there are multiple veneers made of such materials as bamboo weave, sanded, finished and crushed bamboos, banana bark, rattan and lauhala, to name a few.

The ideas are limited only by your imagination. Paneling can be transformed into tropical bar tops and facings, table tops and cabinet-door inserts, as well as ceiling and wall paneling, shelving veneer, free-standing screens, and just about anything you can think of to enhance the beauty of your home. Half-rounds of bamboo measuring from one to two and a half inches make perfect trim to conceal seams.

To cut through single-ply paneling, use a heavy-duty pair of shears. Thicker plies need to be cut with a skilsaw or table saw. Paneling can be affixed to surfaces with mastic, contact cement, adhesive or liquid nails. Use a rolling pin or wallpaper roller for even distribution. Another option is to affix the paneling with finish nails.

HOW TO WEATHERPROOF YOUR NATURAL MATERIALS

For sealing and protecting bamboo and other natural materials from the harsh effects of the sun, Sikkens is a top-of-the-line finish that will penetrate the bamboo but still allow any interior moisture to escape. You can spray it on with a low-pressure sprayer and then back-brush it for complete coverage.

Sikkens comes in choices of flat, semi- and high-gloss in various colors. Butternut is a good color for bamboo. For best results, apply three coats on the surface, allowing each coat to cure for 24 hours. For exterior use, you'll probably need to do this every year or so, but you will gain untold longevity from your bamboo if you keep it maintained.

Bars, counters, ceilings and walls are easily transformed into "tiki chic" through the use of decorative panels and bamboo trim. There are many styles to choose from.

Tropical Woods
for Interiors

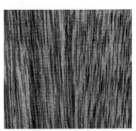

Wood is good. And in Hawaii, nothing offers a home the warmth, richness and exotic appeal of native tropical hardwoods.

Hawaii homeowners have a terrific array of locally grown woods to choose from. Exotic woods like monkeypod, ohia, mango, lychee and eucalyptus are being incorporated in creative new ways in the home. Most of these woods are ideal for flooring, ceilings and paneling, and can be made into veneer and plywood for cabinetry and other applications.

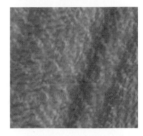

While these secondary local woods are gaining popularity with Island residents, koa remains the most prized of all woods in Hawaii. A limited resource unique to the Islands, koa is also the most expensive.

KOA

No doubt about it, koa is king. Unfortunately, it's pretty much priced out of reach for elaborate home interior applications beyond trim, sills and furniture. That's because Hawaii's once-vast koa forests have been diminished by decades of cattle grazing and harvesting. The wood is scarce, and the days of outfitting your house entirely with koa wood floors and walls are over. It's not only extremely expensive, but today it's considered ostentatious.

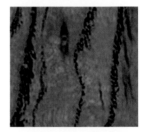

In another 40 years many of the reforested koa trees that grow on the Big Island, Kauai and Maui will be ready for harvest. Currently, the wood is in restricted supply. Even plywood with koa veneer is very expensive.

Primarily a dark wood, koa can sometimes appear white at the outer sapwood. The more curl the grain contains, the more premium the grade. When finished, koa wood is lustrous, rich and beautiful, often imbued with golden reds and browns as well as brown streaks of grain. Because of its primarily deep coloration, though, koa can be a little too "chocolate" if over-utilized architecturally.

It is especially striking when used as an accent in combination with other woods. There are seven grades, the top four of which are only used for making instruments, bowls, boxes and furniture. Natural wood slabs can be transformed into stunning tabletops, counters and bars.

Koa varies in shade, curl and grade—the more curl in the grain, the more premium the grade of koa. When finished, koa can be among the most luminescent of all woods

MANGO

With its luminous, agate-like qualities and interesting grain, mango has become one of Hawaii's most requested native woods. A sleeper wood for years, mango is now being discovered by homeowners for its ability to lighten or "wake up" a room when used for flooring, staircases, walls and cabinetry.

In fact, homeowners are increasingly switching to lighter woods such as mango, especially for ceilings and paneling in high-end homes. Mango is reasonably priced compared to koa and looks terrific on its own or when trimmed with other tropical hardwoods like koa or monkeypod.

Showcasing light and curly colors ranging from mustard yellows, orange reds and lime greens, mango is defined by its wild, streaky grain, which varies in hue from salmon to dark. The attractive black grain patterns result from a natural process called spalting, which occurs when fungus enters the sapwood.

A relatively soft hardwood, mango is susceptible to borer beetles. When cut, it needs to be treated several times during the drying process. When it's turned into flooring, it's treated again to make it effectively bug-proof.

A spiral staircase crafted from mango wood matches the mango-wood flooring below. Mango features a striking amber quality that brings lightness and drama into the home.

Gnarled handrails made of ohia in its natural form are decidedly tropical and sensual. Ohia posts make superb structural supports.

OHIA

Ohia is a distinctly Hawaiian wood that has many creative uses in addition to being a superb material for structural components like posts. Because of its density, it can bear loads much greater than even Douglas fir can support. The beauty of ohia is that while it is utilized structurally, it is also aesthetically pleasing and finely textured.

Ohia trees are associated with Pele, the Hawaiian goddess of the volcano. Often the first signs of life to sprout out of fresh lava flows, the distinctive, crooked trees produce the cherished lehua blossom, official flower of the Island of Hawaii. Usually red in color, the blossoms resemble bottlebrushes.

Ohia makes excellent flooring but is more expensive than mango due to the amount of wood lost during the milling process. When milled, it's a little less stable in the drying stage, resulting in some cracking before it can be turned into flooring.

While most ohia is harvested for posts, it is stunning in its natural form when used for furniture, tables and decorative beams. It can be transformed into rustic pieces such as captain's ladders for lofts and gnarled handrails for stairs, giving your interior a decidedly exotic, Polynesian look.

MONKEYPOD

Along with ohia and mango, monkeypod is among the top three most requested Island-grown woods in Hawaii. A darker wood with light streaks, monkeypod is gaining popularity for use in flooring, cabinets and furniture. Its density is similar to mango's, and it is softer than eucalyptus. It usually has some sapwood at its edges, which makes for a very nice contrast.

Native to South America, monkeypod was introduced to the Islands in the 1800s. The tree can reach towering heights, spreading its thin branches into a large, flowering canopy. A prolific wood, it can be made into veneer and is also available in natural wood slabs.

NORFOLK PINE

Norfolk pine, sometimes called Cook Island pine, is another Island-grown wood that can be made into ceiling and wall paneling. It has a "country" appearance with a tinge of blue in it.

EUCALYPTUS

Grown in dozens of varieties in the Islands, eucalyptus is easy to work with and makes beautiful floors, walls, tables and furniture. Eucalyptus features a quilted, blistered look with a tight, gorgeous grain.

LYCHEE

Denser and lighter in color than eucalyptus, lychee is another spectacular wood when polished. Although it's not as readily available as other woods, lychee can be used for flooring, furniture, inlays and accents. The natural slabs come in smaller sizes and can therefore be fashioned into end tables and small pieces of furniture.

ALBEZIA

A higher-elevation tree, albezia is also known as "chocolate heart." Its look is a cross between koa and monkeypod. Albezia is great for accent moldings, baseboard trim and furniture.

KIAWE

A local wood that grows in abundance, kiawe has a beautiful tight grain and purplish-colored center. Like most of the other tropical woods, kiawe can be purchased in a natural wood slab for making tables and bar tops. Local luthiers are now crafting ukuleles out of kiawe because of its excellent acoustic qualities.

PALM WOOD

Harvested from dormant coconut palms in Asia, palm wood is a bit stronger than bamboo and has a nice look for furniture and flooring.

BAMBOO

Bamboo is a grass, not a wood, but it is as durable as most hardwoods if installed properly. Best of all, it's inexpensive.

Bamboo flooring is becoming extremely popular in Hawaii. The good stuff comes from an area in China near Shanghai called Bamboo Sea, where the bamboo is selectively harvested. Achieving great height and thickness in a short time, it can grow up to two feet a day, making it one of the most renewable resources around.

Bamboo flooring is constructed by laminating three layers of bamboo veneer, glued together under high pressure. Honolulu-based Bamboo Flooring Hawaii LLC offers the natural and carbonized finishes available in a vertical or horizontal cut. The horizontal cut produces a "Tommy Bahama" Hawaiiana look, while the vertical cut yields a more dense, contemporary appearance.

Like most of the other tropical woods, kiawe can be purchased in a natural wood slab for making tables and bar tops.

CREDITS

Front Cover – James Chou Photography (bottom)
Title page – 3 Builders (Macario photo)
Page vi – Macario
Page 2 – Macario
Page 3 – Macario
Pages 4-5 – David Franzen
Page 6 – Graham Builders (Macario photo)
Page 9 – Karen Anderson
Page 10 – 3 Builders (Macario photo)
Page 11 – Macsteel Service Centers USA (Mark Silva photo)
Page 12 – Scott T. Kubo
Page 14 – Macario
Page 15 – Hawaii Home + Remodeling
Page 16 – Homeowners Design Center
Page 17 – Scott T. Kubo
Page 18 – (bedroom) Macario
Page 18 – (mango floor) Karen Anderson
Page 19 – Skylights of Hawaii
Page 20 – Karen Anderson
Page 21 – Coastal Windows
Page 22 – Coastal Windows (both photos)
Page 23 – Coastal Windows
Page 24 – Macario
Page 25 – Macario
Page 26 – Macario
Page 27 – Macario
Pages 28-29 – Landscapes By Tropical Images
Page 30 – Karen Anderson
Page 31 – Mulkern Landscaping (Macario photo)
Page 32 – Eovino & Associates (Macario photo)
Page 33 – Karen Anderson (both photos)
Page 34 – Designed by Cathy O. Lee (Augie Salbosa photo)
Page 35 – Pacific American Lumber
Page 36 – Karen Anderson
Page 38 – Steve's Gardening Service (Macario photo)
Page 39 – Landscapes By Tropical Images
Page 40 – Karen Anderson
Page 41 – (agapanthus) Scott T. Kubo
Page 41 – (gardenia) Scott T. Kubo
Page 41 – (monstera) Scott T. Kubo
Page 41 – (desert rose) David K. Choo
Page 41 – (sagittaria) Landscapes By Tropical Images
Page 41 – (croton) Scott T. Kubo

Page 41 – (gardenia, lower right corner) Landscapes By Tropical Images
Page 42 – Mulkern Landscaping (Macario photo)
Page 43 – Landscapes By Tropical Images
Page 45 – Karen Anderson
Page 46 – Landscapes By Tropical Images
Page 47 – Karen Anderson
Page 48 – Mulkern Landscaping (Macario photo)
Page 49 – Landscapes By Tropical Images
Page 50 – Karen Anderson
Page 51 – Landscapes By Tropical Images
Page 52 – Trex Company
Page 54 – Marblehaus Hawaii
Page 55 – Marblehaus Hawaii
Page 56 – Futura Stone of Hawaii
Page 57 – Kent S. Hwang
Page 59 – Karen Anderson
Page 60 – Futura Stone of Hawaii
Page 63 – www.patterninconcrete.com
Page 64 – Endless Pools
Page 65 – Thomas Deir Studios
Page 66 – Coastal Windows
Page 67 – Landscapes By Tropical Images
Page 68 – Karen Anderson
Page 69 – Karen Anderson
Pages 70-71 – 3 Builders (Macario photo)
Page 72 – Karen Anderson
Page 75 – Karen Anderson
Page 76 – Karen Anderson
Page 77 – Dreamstime.com
Page 78 – Karen Anderson
Page 80 – Skylights of Hawaii
Page 83 – Island Shutters
Page 84 – Karen Anderson
Page 85 – Retractable Screen Solutions (Scott T. Kubo photo)
Page 87 – Retractable Screen Solutions
Page 88 – Retractable Screen Solutions
Pages 90-91 – Dreamstime.com
Page 92 – Dreamstime.com
Page 94 – Karen Anderson
Page 95 – Dreamstime.com
Page 96 – Macario
Page 97 – Francesco Cepolina
Page 99 – Karen Anderson
Page 100 – Dreamstime.com
Page 101 – Dreamstime.com
Page 102 – Kris Anderson

Page 103 – Dreamstime.com
Page 104 – Karen Anderson
Page 106 – U.S. Department of Agriculture
Page 109 – Karen Anderson
Page 110 – Karen Anderson
Page 113 – Kris Anderson
Page 114 – Dreamstime.com
Page 118 – Dreamstime.com
Page 121 – Dreamstime.com
Page 122 – Karen Anderson
Page 124 – Karen Anderson
Page 126 – Karen Anderson
Pages 128-129 – Dreamstime.com
Page 130 – Dreamstime.com
Page 134 – ENERGY STAR
Page 134 – Karen Anderson
Page 135 – Kris Anderson
Page 137 – Karen Anderson
Page 138 – Dreamstime.com
Page 140 – Karen Anderson
Page 141 – Karen Anderson
Page 142 – Karen Anderson
Page 144 – Kris Anderson
Page 145 – Kris Anderson
Page 147 – Karen Anderson
Page 149 – Karen Anderson
Page 151 – Karen Anderson
Page 152 – Dreamstime.com
Page 153 – Hawaiian Island Solar
Page 154 – Hawaiian Electric Company
Page 156 – Karen Anderson (both photos)
Page 157 – Karen Anderson
Pages 162-163 – Macario
Page 164 – Futura Stone of Hawaii
Page 165 – Lokahi Stone
Page 166 – Karen Anderson
Page 167 – Lokahi Stone
Page 168 – Karen Anderson
Page 169 – Rae Huo
Page 170 – Karen Anderson
Page 172 – Karen Anderson
Page 173 – Hawaii Home + Remodeling
Page 174 – Karen Anderson
Page 175 – Karen Anderson
Page 176 – King & Zelko
Page 177 – Scott T. Kubo
Page 178 – Karen Anderson
Page 179 – Karen Anderson
Page 180 – Karen Anderson
Page 181 – (kiawe) Karen Anderson
Page 181 – (bamboo) Scott T. Kubo

MAHALO

First and foremost, thank you to Steve Jones for giving me the idea to write this book. Thanks also to Mom, Kris, Kyle, Christopher and family for your support and encouragement. Special thanks to Malia Scent and Chris Padilla for your valued friendship.

Many thanks also to Linda F. for the lucky pen; Deb Pines and Lori Sceales for the positive words; Nancy Griffith; Delma Kay for the talk stories; Mel Pfeffer; the Kaaloa's at Super Js Authentic Hawaiian Take-Out; and to George Engebretson at Watermark Publishing.

Mahalo very much to: Terry Rollman of *Hawaii Home + Remodeling*, Rob Richard of Blue Rock Masonry, Bruce Richard of Solid Rock Masonry; Jenipher Jones of Horizon Pest Management; Wayne Diamura of The Gas Company; Pam Barrett of Coastal Windows; Mike Souther of ABC Roofing Supply; Steve Jones of Blue Pools of Hawaii; Patricia Macomber of University of Hawaii College of Tropical Agriculture and Human Resources; Kacey Parker of Bamboo Too; Rhett Garon of Pacific Fan Company; Doug Sobaski of Sunlights Hawaii; Jason at Beachside Lighting; Ron Richmond of HECO; Bruce Martin of Martin's Custom Flooring; Steve Johnson of West Hawaii Water Garden Society; Diana Duff of Kona Outdoor Circle; Jeff Long of Long & Associates Architects; Marshall Hickox of The Honolulu Cabinet Company; Roy Bryant of Kona Industries; Deb and Lori of Mamalahoa Hot Tubs & Massage; Andrea Gill of DBEDT; Joylynn Oliveira of Maui Invasive Species Committee; Larry Blatt of Aloha Woods; and to Pips.

Thanks also to Stephanie Amick, Chuck Leslie and Krista Johnson, Elizabeth Eason, Hoku, Sam Geese, Steve and Nora Judd, Colehour and Melanie Bondera, neighbor Chuck, Tess Lusher and Chris Arai, and neighbor Sylvia.

Mahalo to the following, whose assistance was invaluable in researching and writing this book:

ABC Roofing Supply
Airgas Gaspro
Aloha Woods
Bamboo Flooring Hawaii
Bamboo Too
Beaudet Earthworks
Bella Pietra
Big Island Invasive Species
    Committee
Big Rock Manufacturing
Blue Pools of Hawaii
Blue Rock Masonry
Central Pacific Glass
Coastal Windows
Custom Metal Roofing
Dave Johnson, Builder
Davis Tile & Marble
Dr. Fern Duvall, State DLNR
Elizabeth Anderson, Bookkeeper
Farm & Garden
Fowler Painting
Futura Stone
GRK Masonry
Hap Tallman, Heartwood Works
Hawaii Electric Light Company
Hawaii Fumigation
Hawaiian Electric Company

Honolulu Cabinet Company
Honsador Lumber
Horizon Pest Management
HPM Building Supply
Inter-Island Solar Supply Kona
Beachside Lighting
John Kaaloa, Rock-wall Mason
Julian Yates, University of Hawaii
    College of Tropical Agriculture
    and Human Resources
Karen Repan
Kauai Island Utility Cooperative
KCI Kitchen Cabinets
Kona Retractable Screen
    Solutions
Kona Industries
Kona Outdoor Circle
Lady Dee Travel
Long & Associates Architects AIA
Mamalahoa Hot Tubs & Massage
Marblehaus Hawaii
Martin's Custom Flooring
Mary Christ, Realtor
Maui Invasive Species Committee
Maui Electric Company
Michael Clark, HydroShield
Michael Woodbury Home
    Inspection Services

Mildew Man
Pacific American Lumber
Pacific Fan Company
Patricia Macomber, University of
    Hawaii College of Tropical Agri-
    culture and Human Resources
Pools R Us
Reel Things of Hawaii
Rick Elhard, Builder
RSI Roofing and Building Supply
Screens & Things
Soil Plus
SourceTropical
State DBEDT
State Division of Consumer
    Advocacy
State Department of Health
Sunlights Hawaii
The Gas Company
The Screen Shop
Total Eclipse Hawaii Window
    Tinting and Film
Vector Control
Vuick Environmental Consultants
West Hawaii Water Gardening
    Society

INDEX

ABOUT THE AUTHOR

Karen Anderson is a freelance writer living on the island of Hawaii. She is a regular contributor and feature writer for the *West Hawaii Today* newspaper and has also written for *Hawaii* magazine, *Big Island of Hawaii* magazine and the Kona-Kohala Chamber of Commerce. She is currently the managing editor of the monthly magazine, *At Home in West Hawaii*, and was the longtime managing editor of the *Cityline* newspaper in Santa Ana, California.

Along with her dog, Miss Piggy, Karen is also the site manager for Kealakekua Bay Properties in Kona. She enjoys playing guitar and successfully fighting off millipedes and centipedes.

For 25 years, Hawaii's best monthly resource for Island homeowners!

HAWAII TRADE ASSOCIATIONS

Trade associations can help keep you stay up–to-date with the latest technology, assist in finding a contractor, or help with questions or concerns regarding a building or remodeling project. Here's a list of Hawaii-based trade associations and umbrella organizations.

American Institute of Architects, Hawaii Chapter
Founded in 1857, the AIA community of licensed architects helps people understand the importance of architecture in their lives and helps the public learn how to work with architects to realize their visions.
> 119 Merchant St., Suite 402
> Honolulu, HI 96813
> 545-4242
> www.aiahonolulu.org

American Society of Interior Designers, Hawaii Chapter
The Hawaii chapter of this professional designers society promotes ethical practices and design excellence through education, networking and public awareness.
> www.asidhawaii.net

General Contractors Association of Hawaii
Representing its members and acting as their voice in all matters related to the construction industry, the Association provides a full range of services satisfying the needs and concerns of its members, thereby improving the quality of construction and protecting the public interest.
> 1065 Ahua St.
> Honolulu, HI 96819
> 833-1681

Hawaii Flooring Association
This organization of industry professionals provides training, information and consumer assistance.
> 820 Mililani St., Suite 810
> Honolulu, HI 96813
> 537-1224

Hawaii Pest Control Association
The premier authority on pest control in the state of Hawaii, HPCA provides assistance to those seeking solutions to pest control in residential, commercial and industrial environments.

> 820 Mililani St., Suite 810
> Honolulu, HI 96813
> 533-6404
> www.hpca.org

Landscaping Industry Council of Hawaii
As a consortium of professional landscape contractors and architects, the LICH is an umbrella organization representing landscaping trade associations throughout the state.
> P.O. Box 22938
> Honolulu, HI 96823-2938
> info@lichawaii.com
> www.lichawaii.com

National Kitchen and Bath Association, Aloha Chapter
The NKBA's design certifications ensure quality from industry professionals.
> www.nkba.org

Roofing Contractors Association of Hawaii
The RCAH, Hawaii's leading authority for roofing inquiries in the state of Hawaii, was formed to consolidate Hawaii's roofing contractors and to educate consumers as well.
> 820 Mililani St., Suite 810
> Honolulu, HI 96813
> 537-1224
> http://rcah.org/

Subcontractors Association of Hawaii
This umbrella organization encompasses the Hawaii Flooring Association, Roofing Contractors Association of Hawaii, Painting and Decorating Contractors Association of Hawaii, Pacific Electrical Contractors Association, Hawaii Wall & Ceiling Industry Association, Sheet Metal Contractors Association of Hawaii, Hawaii Pest Control Association, and Plumbing & Mechanical Contractors Association of Hawaii. Among other services, the association offers the Public Inspection Program (PIP), a free service to help consumers avoid expensive court costs resulting from contractor issues.
> 820 Mililani St., Suite 810
> Honolulu, HI 96813
> 537-5619

RESOURCES

USEFUL CONTACTS

Animal Quarantine Information

Designed to protect residents and pets from potentially serious health problems associated with the introduction and spread of rabies. All dogs and cats, regardless of age or reason for entry, must comply with Hawaii's import requirements. Contact:

State Department of Agriculture
1428 South King St.
Honolulu, HI 96814-2512
973-9560
www.hawaiiag.org/hdoa/ai_aqs_info.htm

Better Business Bureau of Hawaii

Information on hundreds of companies statewide.

1132 Bishop St., Suite 1507
First Hawaiian Tower
Honolulu, HI 96813-2822
536-6956 or toll-free 877-222-6551

Board of Water Supply

Manages Oahu's municipal water resources and distribution system.

630 S. Beretania St.
Honolulu, HI 96843
748-5050 (information)
748-5460 (water service and new construction)
ContactUs@hbws.org
www.hbws.org/cssweb/

Chamber of Commerce of Hawaii

Works to improve the state's economic climate and to help businesses thrive.

1132 Bishop St., Suite 402
Honolulu, HI 96813
545-4300
www.cochawaii.com

Handbook for the Hawaii Residential Landlord-Tenant Code

Published by the Office of Consumer Protection and the Communications Office of the State Department of Commerce and Consumer Affairs.

586-2634 or toll-free 800-513-8886
www.tenant.net/Other_Areas/Hawaii/lantencd.html

Hawaii Chapter of the Community Associations Institute

Serves the educational, business, and networking needs of community associations in Hawaii. Members include condominium, cooperative, and planned communty associations as well as those who provide services and products to these associations.

P.O. Box 976
Honolulu, HI 96808
808-488-1133
www.caihawaii.org/

Hawaii Legal Forms

Web site features downloadable forms including contracts, business forms, bills of sale, real estate and landlord/tenant contracts.

www.hawaiilegalforms.com

Hawaii State Civil Defense
Provides a full range of resources to help Hawaii residents prepare for, or respond to, disasters.
> 3949 Diamond Head Rd.
> Honolulu, HI 96816
> 808-733-4300
> www.scd.hawaii.gov/

State Department of Land Utilization
Evaluates zoning waivers, adjustments and variances and also assesses existing, planned or cluster developments and shoreline setback.
> 650 S. King St.
> Honolulu, HI 96813
> 523-4131

State Department of Planning and Permitting
Processes applications for land-use approvals and permits for zoning, land use, construction, building, engineering and subdivisions. The department publishes the brochure "Do I Need a Building Permit?"
> 650 S. King St.
> Honolulu, HI 96813
> 523-4505
> info@honoluludpp.org
> www.honolulupp.org

State Department of Transportation Services
Checks for fences and retaining walls that might interfere with traffic visibility at intersections.
> 650 S. King St.
> Honolulu, HI 96813
> 523-4735 (Traffic Engineering Department)
> www.co.honolulu.hi.us/dts/

State Department of Wastewater Management
Confirms sewer availability and existing sewer easements.
> 1000 Uluhia St., Suite 308
> Kapolei, HI 96707
> 523-4429 (sewer connection permit)

RESOURCES

ENERGY RESOURCES ON THE WEB

ENERGY STAR®
A government-backed program that helps businesses and individuals protect the environment through superior energy efficiency.

www.energystar.gov

Hawaii BuiltGreen
Hawaii BuiltGreen™ is a statewide program that makes it easier for builders and homeowners to design and build energy- and resource-efficient homes. Sponsored by the Building Industry Association of Hawaii, this Web site provides resources for environmentally friendly housing construction and land development.

www.bia-hawaii.com/subpageasp?
section=70

Hawaii State Department of Business, Economic Development and Tourism (DBEDT)
Your local DBEDT office provides plentiful ideas for saving money on your energy bills, energy-saving tips and information on state and federal energy tax credits.

www.hawaii.gov/dbedt

Hawaiian Electric Company
HECO's up-to-date information on rebate programs can help offset the cost of purchasing energy-efficient technologies like solar hot-water heating systems and solar-powered attic vents. The Web site also features a calculator to help you determine the correct size of air conditioner for your room or home.

www.heco.com

Rebuild Hawaii
The Rebuild Hawaii Consortium is a statewide forum established in 1998 to encourage Rebuild America partnerships, utilities, community and private business groups to share information on energy and resource development.

www.state.hi.us/dbedt/ert/rebuild/
index.html

The Home Energy Saver
A Web-based, do-it-yourself energy audit tool that helps you find the best ways to save energy in your home.

http://hes.lbl.gov/

U.S. Department of Energy's "Energy Efficiency and Renewable Energy" For Hawaii
Here you will find news about advances in renewable energy and energy efficiency in the Islands, as well as links to Web sites published by DOE's Office of Energy Efficiency and Renewable Energy (EERE) with specific information for Hawaii.

www.eere.energy.gov/states/state_
specific_information.cfm/state=HI

HAWAII'S LANDLORD-TENANT LAWS

Taxes

In Hawaii, landlords must pay an excise tax of 4.166% for payments received on rental property because it is considered gross revenue. Landlords are allowed to add this additional cost to the base rent, as long as the amount added and the percentage charged are stated and agreed to in the rental agreement. For vacation rentals and temporary lodging, there is a transient accommodation tax of 7.25% on the amount paid by the visitor. Lodging could include rooms, apartments, suites or houses that are occupied for less than 180 consecutive days.

Deposits

In Hawaii, the total amount of all deposits cannot exceed the amount of one month's rent. Landlords are not allowed to impose a general excise tax charge on the security deposit. The landlord is not required to pay interest on security deposits. Final move-out inspections are not required in Hawaii, but landlords should do so to avoid disputes.

Rent

There is no rent control in Hawaii, but a landlord must give a tenant adequate written notice of rent increase.

Handbook

These and other particulars are detailed in a residential landlord-tenant handbook, available for downloading from the Hawaii Department of Commerce and Consumer Affairs' Web site at:

www.hawaii.gov/dcca/areas/ocp/
landlord_tenant/

HOME-MAINTENANCE CHECKLIST

Name of Job	Frequency
AIR CONDITIONING	
❏ Replace filter	M
❏ Cleaning and maintenance	6M
INTERIOR	
❏ Test smoke alarms	6M
❏ Check fire extinguisher charge	6M
❏ Inspect washing machine hose connections	Y
❏ Inspect dryer vent	Y
❏ Seal natural stone flooring	Y
❏ Clean out closets to prevent mildew	Y
❏ Inspect for bug entry points	6M
OUTDOOR	
❏ Seal natural stone deck	Y
❏ Seal bamboo structures/fences	Y
❏ Inspect propane tiki torch orifice	6M
❏ Change irrigation timer during rainy season	Y

Name of Job	Frequency
POOL	
❏ Vacuum	W
❏ Chlorine	W
❏ Clean skimmer basket	W
❏ Check chemistry levels	W
❏ Turn off auto-fill to check for leaks	M
❏ Backwash filter	M
SCREENS	
❏ Remove and hose down	6M
SOLAR HOT WATER	
❏ Flush storage tank	Y
❏ Inspect system for leaks	Y
❏ Clean collector glass	Y
❏ Check for corroded parts	Y
❏ Replace anode rod	5Y

W- Weekly   M- Monthly   Q- Quarterly   6M- 6 months   Y- Yearly   5Y- 5 Years

Name of Job	Frequency

SPA

❑ Check chemistry   W

❑ Drain and refill spa   Q

STRUCTURAL

❑ Check exposed wood for signs
of rot or insect damage   6M

❑ Check roof for signs of leaks, rot,
debris, mildew   6M

❑ Clean gutters and downspouts   6M

❑ Cut back trees or branches
touching side of house or roof   6M

❑ Check for signs of spalling
and corrosion   Y

WINDOWS

❑ Check for corrosion   Y

❑ Silcone lube in tracks and
mechanical parts   Y

❑ Check for rot in sills   Y

❑ Check for tight seal   Y

W- Weekly   M- Monthly   Q- Quarterly   6M- 6 months   Y- Yearly   5Y- 5 Years

RESOURCES

BUILDING PERMITS

When you need a bulding permit:

- To erect, construct, alter, remove or demolish any building or structure (including fences, retaining walls and swimming pools)

- For any electrical or plumbing work

- To construct or alter any sidewalk, curb or driveway in public rights-of-way

When you don't:

- To add curbs, planter boxes, and retaining walls and fences not more than 30" high

- To install individual residential television and radio antennas

- Painting, cabinetwork and floor covering

- To build tool and storage sheds not exceeding 120 square feet as accessories to dwellings

- Repairs using similar or the same materials for the purpose of maintenance and which are not more than $1,000 in valuation in any 12-month period, and do not affect any electrical or plumbing installations

Where to apply:

Your local department of planning and permitting

What to bring:

Four sets of plans

For owner-builders:

Homeowners who wish to build or renovate their own homes must register for an owner-builder permit at their nearest county building office. The permit allows the homeowners to act in the role of general contractor and oversee the work of hired subcontractors. As acting employers, homeowners must:

- Provide temporary disability, unemployment and workers' compensation insurance

- Follow employment-tax laws

- Make sure that all hired subcontractors are licensed

When you apply for a permit, you are asked to identify all subcontractors who will be working on the project, specifically the electrical and plumbing contractors. These subcontractors must be licensed. The structure cannot be sold or leased or offered for sale or lease until one (1) year after completion of construction. If a person obtains an owner-builder exemption more than once within a two-year period, that person is presumed under the law to be in violation of the exemption requirements, which could result in costly fines.

County Contacts:

Building Department
City & County of Honolulu
Ground Floor, Municipal Office Building
650 South King Street
523-4505

Building Permits Section
County Land Use & Code Administration
250 South High Street
Wailuku, Maui HI 96793
270-7250

Building Division
County Department of Public Works
4444 Rice Street, Suite 175
Lihue, Kauai HI 96766
241-6655

Building Division
County Department of Public Works
25 Aupuni Street, Room 106
Hilo, Hawaii 96720
961-8331

SOURCE: Hawaii Department of Commerce &
Consumer Affairs www.hawaii.gov/dcca/

RESOURCES

HOW TO HIRE A CONTRACTOR

PRE-QUALIFY THE BIDDER

❏ Review at least three written bids or estimates after providing drawings and plans to the contractors.

❏ Be wary if a bid is significantly less than other bids. It could mean that the contractor did not include all of your requested work.

❏ Conduct background checks and talk to references before hiring.

❏ Before signing any contract or applying for a building permit, be sure that the contractor is licensed in the proper category.

❏ To hear a complaint history about a specific contractor, or to find out if the contractor is licensed, contact the Consumer Resource Center at 587-3222.

CAREFULLY REVIEW THE WRITTEN CONTRACT FOR

❏ Lien rights of all parties involved

❏ Percentage of work that will be subcontracted

❏ Contractor's classification and license number

❏ Whether or not the contractor is bonded

❏ Exact dollar amount that you agreed to pay the contractor

❏ Date that the work should begin and the number of days for completion

❏ Materials to be used

❏ Percentage of work to be subcontracted

❏ Statement of the risk of loss of any payments made to the contractor

SIGN THE CONTRACT

❑ If you still have concerns, consult an attorney to clear up any questions.

❑ If the job is big, consider a completion or performance bond, which guarantees that your construction job will be completed.

AFTER THE SIGNING

❑ Have complete plans showing exactly what will be built and a complete set of specifications related to the drawn plans.

❑ You may want to have a licensed engineer or architect look at the documents.

❑ Keep a file of all work related to your project.

❑ Check your records against lien releases from subcontractors or material suppliers.

❑ Keep changes to contracts or specifications to a minimum, but if you do change orders, make sure they are written.

THROUGHOUT THE PROCESS

❑ Regularly review the contractor's work, especially as it nears completion.

❑ Do a final assessment.

TO FILE A COMPLAINT ABOUT A CONTRACTOR

❑ Contact Consumer Resource Center (808) 587-3222

SOURCE: Contractors License Board, Regulated Industries Complaints Office (RICO), Hawaii Department of Commerce & Consumer Affairs

WHY A LICENSED CONTRACTOR?

Qualifying Contractors

Unlicensed contractors—those who operate without workers' compensation, liability insurance or a Hawaii state government-issued license—comprise as much as 20 percent of the overall construction activity in Hawaii. But simply having a General Excise Tax license and charging less than the going rate doesn't qualify a contractor to handle your job. Here's why:

- A licensed contractor has been evaluated by the State of Hawaii's Contractor's License Board and has the necessary training, experience and qualifications to hold a contractor's license.

- Licensed contractors carry worker's compensation and liability insurance. This protects the homeowner if anyone is injured on site during the job or if any items are damaged while the work is being done.

- Licensed contractors are able to obtain and sign building permits.

- Only a licensed electrical or plumbing contractor can sign building permits for electrical or plumbing work.

- You can do a background check on a licensed contractor through different trade organizations or through the Department of Commerce and Consumer Affairs' Consumer Resource Center.

- The Contractor's Recovery Fund is available to you if anything goes wrong with your project.

The Contractors Recovery Fund

What happens when a homeowner is dissatisfied with the work of a licensed contractor, or if a licensed contractor defaults on an agreement with the homeowner? The Hawaii State Contractors License Board offers a service called the Contractors Recovery Fund. This fund—comprised of fees collected from licensed contractors—allows homeowners to recover up to $12,500 per contract on any judgment declared against a licensed contractor.

Here's how it works: the homeowner files a court action against the licensed contractor. The owner then notifies the License Board about the court action. If a judgment is filed against the contractor, and he does not have the means to pay off the judgment, the homeowner files a claim against the Contractors Recovery Fund. The License Board will pay up to $25,000 for claims against the same licensed contractor. If payments exceed more than $25,000, the board may issue a pro-rata payment.

The recovery fund is the last resort; more often, the homeowner and licensed contractor can settle the dispute themselves. Still, the fund is another sensible reason for homeowners to hire a licensed contractor.

SOURCE: Department of Commerce & Consumer Affairs, Contractors License Board

The Licensing Process

Not all contracting jobs require licenses. A license is not needed if 1) the job does not require a building permit, or 2) the contract price for labor, taxes and materials does not exceed $1,000.

A license is required for all electrical and plumbing jobs that need permits.

Also, homeowners who renovate their own homes don't necessarily need a license. Instead, they are required to register for an owner-builder permit, which allows homeowners to 1) act as their own general contractors and/or 2) hire licensed contractors.

The licensing process is administered by the Contractors License Board, the 13-member board operating under the auspices of DCCA. Licenses are renewed by September 30 of every even year and range anywhere from $160 to $275. New applicants must submit requests for a license by the 20th of every month. They also must pay $50 for the application, an exam fee of $60 and license fees ranging from $255 to $545.

There are three types of licenses issued in Hawaii:

- General engineering contracting: This license is for builders of harbors, tunnels, water and power structures and highways.

- General building contracting: This allows contractors to build structures requiring two or more unrelated specialties, such as signage and lighting.

- Specialty contracting: There are more than 80 specialty categories, from window tinting and landscaping to tiling and laying carpet.

RESOURCES

DISASTER PREPAREDNESS

IN CASE OF FLOOD

Flood Preparedness:
- Avoid building in a floodplain unless you elevate and reinforce your home.

- Elevate the furnace, water heater and electric panel if susceptible to flooding.

- Install "check valves" in sewer traps to prevent floodwater from backing up into the drains of your home.

During a Flood:
- Secure your home. If you have time, bring in outdoor furniture. Move essential items to an upper floor.

- Turn off utilities at the main switches or valve if necessary. Disconnect electrical appliances. Do not touch electrical equipment if you are wet or standing in water.

- If you have to walk in water, walk where the water is not moving. Use a stick to check the firmness of the ground in front of you.

- Do not drive into flooded areas. If flood waters rise around your car, abandon the car and move to higher ground if you can do so safely.

On the Road:
- Be aware of streams, drainage channels, canyons, and other areas known to flood suddenly.

- Six inches of water will reach the bottom of most passenger cars, causing loss of control and possible stalling.

- A foot of water will float many vehicles.

- Two feet of rushing water can carry away most vehicles.

IN CASE OF TSUNAMI

- Turn on your radio to learn if there is a tsunami warning if an earthquake occurs and you are in a coastal area.

- Noticeable water recession from the shoreline is nature's tsunami warning. Move to higher ground immediately.

- Stay out of flooded and damaged areas until officials say it is safe to return.

- Stay away from debris in the water; it may pose a safety hazard to boats and people.

IN CASE OF VOLCANIC ERUPTION

- Evacuate immediately to avoid flying debris, fumes, lateral blast, and lava flow.

- Be aware of mudflows near stream channels.

- Avoid river valleys and low-lying areas.

- Wear long-sleeved shirts and long pants. Use goggles and wear eyeglasses instead of contact lenses.

- Use a dust mask or hold a damp cloth over your face to help with breathing.

- Stay away from areas downwind from the volcano.